WRITE. PRAY. REPEAT.

DAILY DECREE
PRAYER & COLORING JOURNAL

BRENDA KUNNEMAN

DESTINY IMAGE® PUBLISHERS, INC.

P.O. Box 310, Shippensburg, PA 17257-0310

"Publishing cutting-edge prophetic resources to supernaturally empower the body of Christ"

This book and all other Destiny Image and Destiny Image Fiction books are available at Christian bookstores and distributors worldwide.

For more information on foreign distributors, call 717-532-3040.

Reach us on the Internet: www.destinyimage.com.

ISBN 13 TP: 978-0-7684-7456-5

For Worldwide Distribution, Printed in the U.S.A.

1 2 3 4 5 6 7 8 / 27 26 25 24 23

CONTENT

YOUR ENERGY IS RENEWED!

DECREE

Today, in the spirit of divine agreement, we decree that your youth is being renewed like the eagle. You shall run and not grow weary and you will walk and not faint. Together, we speak over you energy, vitality, life, and longevity. We break off your life the effects of lethargy, exhaustion, and fatigue. We say that all your emotional and bodily functions, systems, hormones, cells, and organs operate properly as they were created by God and shall not cause you to be tired or worn out. We bind up all stress-causing circumstances that would make you weary and we say that they are replaced by seasons of joy unspeakable and full of glory. Right now we declare that the life of God flows through your entire being in a fresh new way and revitalized energy rests upon you now! Amen!

SCRIPTURE

But they that wait upon the Lord shall renew their strength; they shall mount up with wings as eagles; they shall run, and not be weary; and they shall walk, and not faint (Isaiah 40:31).

JOURNAL

What is one area of your life where you need supernatural energy? Journal it below and trust Him to fill you to overflowing!

_____

_____

_____

_____

_____

_____

_____

_____

The life of God flows through my entire being in a fresh new way!

VIRTUE AND GOD'S PRESENCE UPON YOU!

DECREE

Today we decree together that you experience encounters with God's tangible presence. We say that your mind, heart, and physical being feels and senses the power of the Almighty. May your bones be filled with supernatural life. We call upon the Lord to touch you in an unusual way and that a fresh anointing comes upon you. May the hand of God be upon you everywhere you go. We say that every place you walk this day the glory of the Lord shall go before you, stand beside you, and also be your protection from behind. Even as the anointing of the Lord was with Jesus, so shall that same anointing be upon you. We prophesy that heavenly gifts shall rest upon you and that you are enabled to manifest the Kingdom of heaven in all your circles of influence. We declare right now that you shall surely say, "The presence of the Lord follows me, is here with me and upon me!" Amen!

SCRIPTURE

How God anointed Jesus of Nazareth with the Holy Ghost and with power: who went about doing good, and healing all that were oppressed of the devil; for God was with him (Acts 10:38).

JOURNAL

Make a list of the places you will go today, and write a prayer inviting God to surprise you with encounters in any and every one of these places.

_____

_____

_____

_____

_____

_____

_____

Heavenly gifts
shall rest upon me and
I am enabled to manifest
the Kingdom of heaven!

DIVINELY SET UP

DECREE

Today we decree you come into the place of a divine setup. We decree right now that you begin to see the Lord arranging, rearranging, shifting, and changing circumstances for your good. We say right now that your eyes are opened to see that God is at work in the most difficult situations. We call for a divine revelation to come upon you, enabling you to see the myriad of angels moving on your behalf at this very moment. We declare that you are able to see God setting things in order. We break the power of setback and decline. We command every spirit of hindrance and resistance to be bound in Jesus' Name. We call upon the Lord to make the way so you can go forward in victory and that all things shall work out and turn out well. Right, now we prophesy you are being divinely set up to prosper and succeed! Amen!

SCRIPTURE

And we know that all things work together for good to them that love God, to them who are the called according to his purpose (Romans 8:28).

JOURNAL

What challenge are you facing right now that you can't see a solution for? Journal it and give God full access to break into this situation unexpectedly.

_____

_____

_____

_____

_____

_____

_____

_____

My eyes are opened to see that God is at work in my most difficult situations.

DELIVERANCE FROM THE ARROWS

DECREE

Today we decree that you are covered by God's mighty angelic forces and delivered from every arrow of the enemy. We prophesy no weapon formed against you shall prosper. We say every diabolical scheme, plot, or plan of the enemy is stopped and interrupted by warring angels and God's power, and every attack must fall to the ground. We say you are delivered from the terror by night and from the arrow that flies by the day. Every pestilence that walks in darkness around you is stopped. We declare no witchcraft curse, no demonic spell, no work of divination, no incantation or hex will have any effect on you and is rendered entirely powerless in the authority of Jesus' Name! And, right now we say every attack is replaced with peace and calm. We say blessing overtakes you and brings all chaos into divine order. We prophesy that you dwell in safety, for the Lord is your refuge. Angels are bearing you up in their hands this day and long life and salvation are upon you! Amen!

SCRIPTURE

Do not be afraid of the terrors of the night, nor the arrow that flies in the day (Psalm 91:5 NLT).

JOURNAL

What is one place where you have been hit by the enemy's arrows in the past? Write a prayer asking God to place His angels on guard for you in this area.

_____

_____

_____

_____

_____

_____

QUESTIONS ANSWERED

Decree

Today we decree that you receive answers to important questions, concerns, and thoughts. We say that insights from heaven come upon you to bring clarity and understanding. We break the power of all confusion, bewilderment, and clutter within your mind. We declare that all sense of misunderstanding or delusion cannot enter any part of your being, and we break the power of every evil spirit of error in the Name of Jesus. We pray that the Lord's peace rests upon you regarding those questions which only heaven can reveal in God's timing, and that a renewed trust in the guidance of your heavenly Father prevails. We say that your joy abounds above any sense of despair and that you are overshadowed by the truth that the Lord is always working on your behalf and is fighting for you! Amen!

Scripture

I will instruct you and teach you in the way you should go; I will counsel you with my loving eye on you (Psalm 32:8 NIV).

Journal

Ask God a question you need an answer to and journal it below. Nothing is beyond Him! Journal the answer He provides when it comes.

My joy abounds above any sense of despair!

RISE UP AS AN OVERCOMER!

DECREE

Today we decree that you live as an overcomer and that defeat can never have a hold over you. We break the power of any cloud of failure that might exist over you and we say it is replaced by overwhelming success. We declare you are well able to rise above difficulty and struggle coming against your mind, body, family, occupation, and finances. We speak that you operate in the strength of the Lord and power of His might. We say what you put your hand to shall prosper. You are the head and not the tail, you are above and not beneath, and no weapon formed against you shall prosper. We declare that you rise up today, that you overcome and stand strong in the power and grace of God upon you! Amen!

SCRIPTURE

Now thanks be unto God, which always causeth us to triumph in Christ, and maketh manifest the savour of his knowledge by us in every place (2 Corinthians 2:14).

JOURNAL

What mountain are you facing that you need to overcome? Write it down, then cross it out and write JESUS over it! Then write a prayer thanking Him for giving you His victory.

_____

_____

_____

_____

_____

_____

_____

_____

I am well able to rise above difficulty and struggle coming against my mind, body, family, occupation, and finances.

DEDICATION RENEWED; CONDEMNATION BROKEN

DECREE

Today we decree that all areas of struggle, sin, iniquity, offense, and every generational curse is broken from your life. We say all negative or poor habits are removed and that a renewed consecration to the Lord rests upon you. We pray you have the strengthened faith to release all areas of weakness, failure, and feebleness before the foot of the cross. May you walk in the vast measure of liberty and forgiveness in Christ Jesus. We bind every spirit of the enemy from bringing condemnation, guilt, or shame, and we decree that you receive a full cleansing by the Word of God upon your entire being—spirit, soul, and body. May all worldly and earthly burdens be removed and may you take upon you the light and easy burden of Christ. May you live in a renewed and refreshed life of holiness and dedication to Jesus, and may your joy be both restored and made full in Him! Amen!

SCRIPTURE

There is therefore now no condemnation to them which are in Christ Jesus, who walk not after the flesh, but after the Spirit (Romans 8:1).

JOURNAL

Today, write briefly about your first experience of salvation and dedicating yourself to the Lord. Jesus loves this beautiful moment you share!

_____

_____

_____

_____

_____

_____

All negative or poor habits are removed and a renewed consecration to the Lord rests upon me.

DECLARING SAME-DAY MIRACLES!

DECREE

Today we decree that you receive sudden answers to prayer. We declare that same-day miracles rest upon you. We say that you enter the season when things that have taken years and months will immediately manifest on the same day you pray. We prophesy that you receive your daily bread on *this* day! We break the power of every hindrance and blockage from the enemy in Jesus' Name! We bind the power of every attack that would come to defeat your faith and confidence. We bind weariness of mind and we loose hope and renewed zeal. We say the season of open doors, successes, blessings, favor, manifestation, opportunity, and increase rests upon you! We declare an end to decrease and we call for same-day miracles and immediate answers to prayer to break forth on every side right now! Amen!

SCRIPTURE

Give us this day our daily bread (Matthew 6:11).

JOURNAL

Write down a miracle you are asking God to do for you today. Write down today's date and the time, and come back and add the time when the answer arrives.

Today I decree that
I receive sudden
answers to prayer.

A DOUBLE-PORTION ANOINTING!

DECREE

Today we decree a double-portion anointing of God's power to be upon you. According to Isaiah 61:7, we speak that you have a double-portion anointing that replaces your season of shame. We say you receive a doubling of the anointing to prophesy, preach, declare, and pray. We say a tangible double anointing comes upon you to be a witness and to minister the Gospel to others. We pray that you receive a double-portion anointing to pray for the sick, cast out evil spirits, and to walk in signs and wonders. We rebuke all intimidation and say that you stand bold and strong in your authority against the enemy and we decree that your season to shine has come! Right now, we call for a doubling upon the work of your hands to live in success and in God's divine blessing. We say that the level of power and blessing you have walked in up to this point accelerates and doubles immediately! Today we declare double, double, double to rest mightily and powerfully upon you! Amen!

SCRIPTURE

Instead of your shame you will receive a double portion, and instead of disgrace you will rejoice in your inheritance. And so you will inherit a double portion in your land, and everlasting joy will be yours (Isaiah 61:7 NIV).

JOURNAL

What area has God given you special anointing in? Write a prayer asking Him to double that gift.

_____

_____

_____

_____

_____

A double-portion anointing of God's power is upon me.

A WORD IN YOUR MOUTH

DECREE

Today we decree your mouth is filled with divine words. May you be released to declare, prophesy, pray, bind, loose, and sing new songs. Right now we declare that a watch is placed upon your tongue and that you will not speak anything contrary to the Word of the Lord or His promises and statutes. We say that your words are divinely inspired to bless others and that you have a mouth filled with wisdom. May your words also be filled with grace, seasoned with salt so that you know how to give an answer to every person who asks about the hope of the Gospel within you! We say right now in Jesus' Name that you know how to answer hard questions and that you speak with the power and authority of God upon you! We say your words have power and that there is a heavenly word in your mouth! Amen!

SCRIPTURE

Let your speech be always with grace, seasoned with salt, that ye may know how ye ought to answer every man (Colossians 4:6).

JOURNAL

Write a prayer, song, poem, or declaration of love to Jesus today.

I speak with the power and authority of God upon me!

MIGHTY WARRIOR ARISE!

DECREE

Today we decree that you rise up as a mighty warrior of the Spirit like Gideon. We speak a spirit of valor upon you right now! We declare you will not back down from the operations of the enemy that would work to intimidate, manipulate, or control you. We say that you are well equipped to wage war with the weapons of might that will pull down strongholds. We prophesy that you are rooted and grounded in love and that you shall never stumble or become offended by any fiery darts of the wicked. We declare that your faith will not fail. May you be surrounded with assurance and confidence that God is with you and He shall not allow you to fall or be defeated! We say it's so in Jesus' Name!

SCRIPTURE

And the angel of the Lord appeared unto him, and said unto him, The Lord is with thee, thou mighty man of valour (Judges 6:12).

JOURNAL

What is one area in your life where you feel like you are in a battle? Journal it and claim the spirit of valor to come upon you for this fight.

_____

_____

_____

_____

_____

_____

_____

_____

_____

_____

_____

I am well equipped to wage war with weapons of might that pull down strongholds.

YOUR EYES ARE OPEN

DECREE

Today we decree your eyes are open to see what heaven is saying and doing in this important season. We pray that you are filled right now with spiritual wisdom, insight, and understanding. We declare that all spiritual blindness, confusion, deception, and darkness dissipates and that your heart and mind are flooded with light. We prophesy that you have an understanding like the tribe of Issachar to discern the times and seasons. We declare that any ungodly ideologies of the world will not infiltrate or control your beliefs, attitudes, and choices. We break the power of every ungodly soul tie and every lie from the enemy that is preventing you from gaining a righteous perspective. We say today that truth, divine revelation, and perception permeate your being and that nothing shall be able to enter your eye gate that is not from God! We place a boundary around your eyes, ears, and thoughts, and we say today that your eyes are open to see clearly according to the Spirit of the Lord! Amen!

SCRIPTURE

That the God of our Lord Jesus Christ, the Father of glory, may give unto you the spirit of wisdom and revelation in the knowledge of him: the eyes of your understanding being enlightened; that ye may know what is the hope of his calling, and what the riches of the glory of his inheritance in the saints (Ephesians 1:17-18).

JOURNAL

Ask Jesus if there is anything clouding your vision today. Journal it, commit to removing it from your life, and ask Him to show you something you couldn't see before. Write down what you discover.

I declare that all spiritual blindness, confusion, deception, and darkness dissipates and my heart and mind are flooded with light.

DECLARING WHOLENESS

DECREE

Today we are declaring wholeness upon you—spirit, soul, and body. We say that you receive a fresh spiritual impartation from the throne room of heaven. We say that revelation and insight comes to enlighten your eyes in the things of the spirit. We prophesy that your soul is renewed and that your mind, will, emotions, intellect, and memory are touched afresh by the anointing. All mind-binding and invasive demons that would try to control your thoughts are bound and removed from torturing your thinking in the mighty Name of Jesus. We also speak and say that your body receives a divine and tangible touch right now. All pain, disease, infirmity, and chronic health issues are resolved and healed by the power of God because of the stripes of Jesus our Lord and Savior. We decree today that your entire person is made whole from all that is not right and that you are new and renewed in every part of your being!

SCRIPTURE

Thy faith hath made thee whole; go in peace, and be whole of thy plague (Mark 5:34).

JOURNAL

Write down a need you have today, whether large or small, in your body or in your soul. Journal the date and time when God heals you!

I say that revelation and insight comes to enlighten my eyes in the things of the spirit.

YOUR SEASON OF EXPANSION AND ADVANCEMENT!

DECREE

We decree today that you are loosed from a spirit of decay and decline. In the Name of Jesus we break all wicked operations by the princes and powers of the air and rulers of darkness and we say they are cast out from working against you! We decree that reduction is replaced with increase and enlargement. Decline is replaced with improvement, growth, and fruitfulness. Dead dreams are replaced with living, resurrected vision. We prophesy that your sense of purpose is refreshed once again! And, we say that all that has seemed to crumble is rebuilt by God's miraculous hand of power. We declare you are flourishing and a new season of expansion and advancement is upon you!

SCRIPTURE

Enlarge the place of your tent, and let them stretch out the curtains of your habitations; spare not, lengthen your cords, and strengthen your stakes. For you shall spread out to the right hand and to the left, and your descendants shall inherit the nations and make the desolate cities to be inhabited (Isaiah 54:2-3 MEV).

JOURNAL

What is one thing in your life that seems to be going downhill? Write it down, then lift it up to God for a divine turnaround!

I decree today that I am loosed from a spirit of decay and decline.

GOD IS GRANTING YOU BOLDNESS

DECREE

Today we decree that a new level of boldness, confidence, and fierceness for the Word of God and heavenly truths comes upon you. We command all timidity, intimidation, shyness, and fear to depart from you in Jesus' Name! Every lying spirit that would back you into a corner is bound. We say you are bold and confident like a lion to stand up for what you know and you are bold and strong to stand up for Jesus Christ. We say that you are well able to stand in the evil day and that you shall stand steadfastly in the promises, truths, and commands of the Word of God amidst opposition. We say you shall remain firm in faith for all that heaven has provided and taught you. We declare what God has destined for you shall come to pass and that a fresh, new endowment of boldness and assurance shall rest upon you in this season! Amen!

SCRIPTURE

The wicked flee when no man pursues, but the righteous are bold as a lion (Proverbs 28:1 MEV).

JOURNAL

What is one area of your life in which you need boldness? Journal it below in the form of a prayer.

_____

_____

_____

_____

_____

_____

_____

_____

I command all timidity, intimidation, shyness, and fear to depart in Jesus' Name!

FIRE AND PASSION IGNITED

DECREE

Today we decree that your fire and passion is ignited afresh. We declare that the flame of your first love in Christ is rekindled anew. We say that all lethargy is dispersed in Jesus' Name! We declare you receive a fresh baptism of the Holy Spirit and power. May your prayer language be ignited as the first time you prayed in the Spirit. We speak that you are used in the gifts of the Spirit to lay hands upon the sick and they shall recover. We say the prophetic revelation gifts flow through you. May the gifts of power to cast out devils operate freely, and we say that you are ignited to be used by God in in a new way in this season. May souls whom you come in contact with respond to the sound of your voice, and we prophesy that the word of God flowing through you shall not return void!

SCRIPTURE

Then His word was in my heart as a burning fire shut up in my bones (Jeremiah 20:9 MEV).

JOURNAL

Ask God to create an opportunity for you to release a word from Him to someone else. Come back later and write down what happened.

The prophetic revelation gifts flow through me.

PURPOSE AND DESTINY REVIVED

DECREE

Today we decree that you see your destiny and calling through the eyes of the Spirit. We say that you see your purpose with faith. We declare that all clouded vision and blindness that would try to prevent you from seeing your bright future is destroyed in Jesus' Name. We prophesy that your barren season becomes fruitful. We declare that everything you are called to accomplish shall become manifest and that every prophetic word from heaven shall bear fruit. We command all gloominess to clear and we say bright days are before you.

SCRIPTURE

For I know the plans that I have for you, says the Lord, plans for peace and not for evil, to give you a future and a hope (Jeremiah 29:11 MEV).

JOURNAL

Write a prayer of thanksgiving for the destiny God has in store for you. Celebrate with Him as He brings it to fulfillment.

_____

_____

_____

_____

_____

_____

_____

_____

_____

_____

_____

Today I decree that I see my destiny and calling through the eyes of the Spirit.

FREE FROM DISCOURAGEMENT

DECREE

Today we decree that you are loosed from all discouragement. We break the power of every evil spirit of dismay, depression, and disappointment in the authority of Jesus' Name! We declare discouragement is replaced by great encouragement and that good news shall arrive. May the Holy Spirit of comfort and peace fill your soul. We say that your eyes see past the dark clouds and that you see the plan, purpose, and presence of God upon you and around you. We decree you are able to see a good outcome. We declare that no weapon formed against you shall prosper and every tongue that would rise up to accuse you shall be silenced by the power of God. Today, we say that a fresh anointing comes upon you and that your joy is restored to the fullest measure!

SCRIPTURE

Cast your burden on the Lord, and He will sustain you; He will never allow the righteous to be moved (Psalm 55:22 MEV).

JOURNAL

What has discouraged you recently? Journal it, and then journal the comfort and peace Holy Spirit brings to this issue.

_____

_____

_____

_____

_____

_____

_____

_____

I am loosed from all discouragement!

BLESSINGS UPON YOUR HOUSE

DECREE

Today we decree household blessings and salvations. We declare the visitation of God is coming to your house to release household blessings. We pray every member of your family shall be touched by the power and presence of God in a divine way. We break the power of every hindering spirit from coming against your home, family, property, and belongings in the Name of Jesus. We say that all works of darkness are bound. We speak an overshadowing of the Lord over your home and pray that angelic forces shall be released to protect and stand watch. We pray a new day over your home and that in this season every family member in your home comes into a new and fresh encounter with the Lord Himself!

SCRIPTURE

Believe in the Lord Jesus and you will be saved, along with everyone in your household (Acts 16:31 NLT).

JOURNAL

Choose one family member who needs salvation, a renewed passion for Jesus, or a supernatural blessing. Write down your prayer for them today, and remember to add the answer later!

_____

_____

_____

_____

_____

_____

_____

_____

_____

_____

Every family member in my home is coming into a new and fresh encounter with the Lord Himself!

DECLARE A NEW SEASON

DECREE

Today we decree you are divinely transferred into a new and glorious season from the Lord. We command all the cycles of trouble, hindrance, warfare, and disappointment to cease in Jesus' Name. We say a new prophetic declaration is being written over you that places you in a season of peace, prosperity, blessing, and restfulness. We bind the works of darkness from filling your mind with fear and resentment. We break the power of all lethargy and apprehension that arose from the circumstances surrounding the former season and we say you are infused with new seeds of fresh fire, vision, excitement, and faith for what is ahead. We say you are advancing into greater days and that your joy shall be made full! It's your time to shine because a new and brighter season is upon you.

SCRIPTURE

Remember ye not the former things, neither consider the things of old. Behold, I will do a new thing; now it shall spring forth; shall ye not know it? I will even make a way in the wilderness, and rivers in the desert (Isaiah 43:18-19).

JOURNAL

What new season are you embracing? Write it down. If you don't know, write a prayer asking for God's blessing during the next transition, and commit to staying flexible.

_____

_____

_____

_____

_____

_____

_____

I am divinely transferred into a new and glorious season from the Lord.

DECREE OVER YOUR OCCUPATION AND BUSINESS

DECREE

Today we decree over you regarding your job, business, and occupation. We are asking the Lord to set up divine connections, interactions, events, appointments, and God-encounters. May you be able to interact with people of influence to help set you up for success. We declare open doors, interviews, contacts, contracts, new clients, and customers. We speak that raises, bonuses, tips, and commissions will come into your hands speedily. We declare promotions and awards for a job well done. We prophesy favor when you come in and when you go out. We declare you receive fresh ideas that create acceleration and advancement. We say that you will not be ignored, declined, passed over, or left out in Jesus' Name because you are the head and not the tail, above only and not below. Today we say that you are gainfully and steadily employed and that success and blessing shall be your portion!

SCRIPTURE

The Lord will send a blessing on your barns and on everything you put your hand to. The Lord your God will bless you in the land he is giving you (Deuteronomy 28:8 NIV).

JOURNAL

Write down one area of your occupation where you especially need to invite the presence of Jesus today.

_____
_____
_____
_____
_____

I declare open doors,
interviews, contacts, contracts,
new clients, and customers.

BINDING UP WEARINESS

DECREE

Today we break the power of all weariness in Jesus' Name! We say that every evil entity from the enemy is rendered powerless to steal your resolve and rob you of your determination. We call upon the heavenly hosts to be released and wage war on your behalf. We pray the Lord supplies you with supernatural strength so that you can stand your ground. You will mount up with eagle's wings, run and not grow weary, you will walk and not faint, and we say you are completely overshadowed with faith and power! You shall not become tired in well doing. You will stay the course and finish all that heaven has given you to do without giving up or giving in to pressure. We declare your harvest shall not be stolen from you in Jesus' Name!

SCRIPTURE

Let us not become weary in doing good, for at the proper time we will reap a harvest if we do not give up (Galatians 6:9 NIV).

JOURNAL

What upcoming task or event do you anticipate will make you weary, tired, or exhausted? Write it, bring it before God, and come back after and journal how He carried you through.

UNDOING HEAVY BURDENS!

DECREE

Right now, we decree that you are released and free from every heavy burden that is trying to weigh you down. We say that you receive the light and easy yoke of Christ that enables you to rise up and live in wholeness, freedom, peace, and joy. In the Name of Jesus we bind up every lie of the enemy that would make you believe that you will never come out from under the weight of affliction! We command all demonic oppression to come off of you. We say that according to Nahum 1:9, your season of affliction must end and it shall not rise a second time and whom the Son sets free is free indeed. We declare relief, alleviation, and deliverance from the burden created by the demands of life. We speak this over you and say it manifests and rests upon you now!

SCRIPTURE

Then Jesus said, "Come to me, all of you who are weary and carry heavy burdens, and I will give you rest. Take my yoke upon you. Let me teach you, because I am humble and gentle at heart, and you will find rest for your souls. For my yoke is easy to bear, and the burden I give you is light" (Matthew 11:28-30 NLT).

JOURNAL

Draw a cross. Write down the name of something that is burdening you—put it on the cross, draw nails to keep it there, and thank Jesus for taking this burden from you!

In the Name of Jesus I bind up every lie of the enemy that I will never come out from under the weight of affliction!

INVADING FEAR MUST GO!

DECREE

Today we *decree* that any form of fear trying to invade your life is bound up in the Name of Jesus! We come against all financial fear and say that every monetary need is met this year. We bind all fear regarding your family and loved ones. We say they are protected by God's angelic hosts. We decree that all fear of death and tragedy is bound and destroyed! We bind the fear of sickness and disease. We say that every fear of failure, rejection, oppression, and depression must leave you right now! We break off all fear of the future concerning the nations and world events and we declare these things shall have no ability to torment your mind. You are favored and blessed of God and *all* shall be well concerning you! We agree on this together in faith, in Jesus' mighty Name!

SCRIPTURE

Don't be afraid, for I am with you. Don't be discouraged, for I am your God. I will strengthen you and help you. I will hold you up with my victorious right hand (Isaiah 41:10 NLT).

JOURNAL

Journal a fear you had in the past that you have victory over now. Then journal a present fear, and write down how you will look at that issue with Jesus on your side.

I decree that all fear of death and tragedy is bound and destroyed!

BINDING UP TROUBLING SPIRITS

DECREE

We declare this shall be a day filled with God's grace, blessings, goodness, and mercy. We bind all harassing and troubling works of the enemy in Jesus' Name and say that all frustration, bad news, disappointment, letdown, discouragement, aggravation, and disturbances have no place in your day. We prophesy that you will not have to hassle with annoying moments that steal from the joy of the day and meddle with your plans and schedule. Angelic forces are being released so that you are protected and nothing shall harm or injure you. We take authority over evil spirits that would cause family troubles and strife, breakdowns and setback, and we say this will be a day filled with peace, fun, and joy! All shall be well this day, this week, month, and year! We speak it in Jesus' Name! Amen!

SCRIPTURE

Then the people of the land weakened the hands of the people of Judah, and troubled them in building (Ezra 4:4).

JOURNAL

What troubles you lately? Write a note to the Lord about how you see Him delivering you from this attack. Thank Him for keeping it far away from you!

_____

_____

_____

_____

_____

_____

_____

I declare this shall be a day filled with God's grace, blessings, goodness, and mercy.

HOPE RESTORED!

DECREE

Today, we decree that your hope is restored and springs forth as a tree of life. We say that every delay is converted into acceleration. We prophesy that every setback becomes a setup for something greater than you dreamed. We break the spirit of delay and say you receive a new sense of anticipation and confidence. We pray that blessings, increase, and fullness will break loose and overflow upon you for this current season. We speak to your future and destiny and declare that all God has planned for you cannot be aborted by the enemy in Jesus' Name and good things will begin to manifest before you! It's a season of good. Take it, it's yours!

SCRIPTURE

Hope deferred maketh the heart sick: but when the desire cometh, it is a tree of life (Proverbs 13:12).

JOURNAL

Write a note to Jesus asking Him if there is any place where you have lost hope. Write His answer, then receive a new surge of hope in this area.

Good things are manifesting
before me! It's a season of good.

PROPHETIC INSIGHT

DECREE

Today we declare you receive wisdom and prophetic insight for everything you do today and for every decision you must make. We say your spiritual ears are open to what heaven is saying to you with pinpoint accuracy. May the heart, mind, and intent of God be downloaded into your spirit. May you experience prophetic visions and dreams. We prophesy that you hear the secrets of God. We break off any deaf and dumb spirits that would come to disrupt your spiritual hearing and knowing. We declare you will not receive, hear, or communicate anything that is not of God. We break the power of confusion and misinformation from coming against your mind and declare all voices not from God cannot interfere. We speak now that your prophetic spirit is alive and active to know what is of God and that you are able to speak for Him with precision in Jesus' Name!

SCRIPTURE

The eyes of your understanding being enlightened; that ye may know what is the hope of his calling, and what the riches of the glory of his inheritance in the saints (Ephesians 1:18).

JOURNAL

Today, write a prayer to your Heavenly Father asking Him for His wisdom insight—but leave a blank for Him to fill in what He wants to show you.

_____

_____

_____

_____

_____

_____

_____

I experience prophetic visions and dreams.

JOY IN KNOWING HIM!

DECREE

Today we declare that you experience the renewed joy of knowing Jesus. May you know Him and the power of His resurrection. May you know and receive His great love. We declare you have revelation of His tangible anointing upon you. We pray you have revelation knowledge in Him that provides you wisdom, direction, and understanding. We pray that you experience a fresh excitement about spiritual things. May your divine knowledge of the Lord enable you to have assurance of His faithfulness and grace resting over your life. We declare right now that every spirit of fear and confusion is bound, and we say that your awareness of the Lord's presence takes precedence in your thoughts. We declare you sense God upon you and around you all day in Jesus' glorious Name!

SCRIPTURE

Restore unto me the joy of thy salvation (Psalm 51:12).

JOURNAL

What is something you can do that evokes a sense of the Lord's joy inside? Journal it and ask for His supernatural joy to fill you!!

I sense God upon me and around me all day in Jesus' glorious Name!

ANOINTED AND APPOINTED!

DECREE

Today we decree over you that you are called by God. You are anointed and appointed for a divine purpose to accomplish something fruitful and lasting. We prophesy a fresh anointing for heavenly service comes upon you. Like Jesus, we say you are empowered to go about doing good and setting people free from oppression. We declare you will impact lives in a divine way. We bind the works of the enemy to devalue you and try to pull you into lethargy or a place that is void of purpose. We say that your goals are defined and ordained from heaven and may all you set your hand to do prosper. May you accomplish more this year and do more for the Kingdom of God than ever before. Let divine doors be opened before you that will bring you before people of influence that you might affect them with the anointing. We declare it in Jesus' Name!

SCRIPTURE

How God anointed Jesus of Nazareth with the Holy Ghost and with power: who went about doing good, and healing all that were oppressed of the devil; for God was with him (Acts 10:38).

JOURNAL

What appointment has God already given you? What has He anointed you to accomplish? Write it down, then ask Him to take you into the next level of this anointing.

_____

_____

_____

_____

_____

_____

Today I decree that I am called by God.

RESTORATION AND PAYBACK!

Decree

Today we decree that you experience restoration from the years the locust and cankerworm have eaten. May everything that has seemed to have decayed or crumbled be reestablished into newness, and may you begin to flourish again. In the spirit, we prophesy a rebuilding of the old waste places and that streams begin to flow in the desert. We break the power of destruction, attack, and devastation in Jesus' Name. We pray that you begin to receive restitution, payback, benefits, and reimbursements. We pray that fruitfulness will remain in your life and that you will experience fulfillment, success, and complete contentment. We ask that all that God has planned for your life will begin to fully manifest in this season before you! We speak all of this in Jesus' Name.

Scripture

And I will restore to you the years that the locust hath eaten, the cankerworm, and the caterpiller, and the palmerworm, my great army which I sent among you. And ye shall eat in plenty, and be satisfied, and praise the name of the Lord your God, that hath dealt wondrously with you: and my people shall never be ashamed (Joel 2:25-26).

Journal

Write down 3 situations that you would consider to be a loss in your life and how you see God restoring you and paying you back for what the enemy stole from you!

_____

_____

_____

_____

_____

All that God has planned for my life will begin to fully manifest in this season before me!

MENTAL OPPRESSION IS BOUND

DECREE

Today we decree you overcome all manner of fatigue that may be trying to set you back. We bind tiredness, physical exhaustion, mental oppression, and emotional stress. May the fear and distress of this world be far from you, and we bind all manner of doom, depression, and downheartedness in the Name of Jesus. We say anxiety has no place near you. We call for angels to surround you, and may the peace of the Holy Spirit give you the assurance that all is well and good things shall be your portion! We declare you experience calm, peace, and tranquility. We declare comfort, contentment, and complete relief in your mind that shall cause you to smile and rejoice. We decree all is well and shall be well! Amen!

SCRIPTURE

Looking unto Jesus the author and finisher of our faith; who for the joy that was set before him endured the cross, despising the shame, and is set down at the right hand of the throne of God. For consider him that endured such contradiction of sinners against himself, lest ye be wearied and faint in your minds (Hebrews 12:2-3).

JOURNAL

What is one area in your life where you experience mental difficulty and oppression? Write it down and see that specific struggle laid upon Jesus on the cross. Now claim your victory in this area!

_____

_____

_____

_____

_____

_____

_____

I call for angels to surround me and the peace of the Holy Spirit to give me the assurance that all is well and good things are my portion!

DIVINE REVERSAL!

DECREE

Today we decree divine reversal! We say that discouragement turns into encouragement, setbacks become increase, fear becomes faith, and all lack turns into surplus. We declare that sickness becomes health and fatigue is replaced by energy and life. We declare that hindrances move out of the way and are replaced by breakthrough and results. We declare that every question becomes an answer and that all areas of confusion turn into clarity. We decree that strife becomes unity and frustration turns into success. We say all things that have been negatively set into motion are now completely reversed! May all that concerns you experience a complete and total divine reversal and turnaround from heaven in Jesus' mighty Name!

SCRIPTURE

The Lord shall cause thine enemies that rise up against thee to be smitten before thy face: they shall come out against thee one way, and flee before thee seven ways (Deuteronomy 28:7).

JOURNAL

Today, write down a situation you are facing that has seemed to have gone extremely wrong. Write a prayer to the Father asking for His help and that expresses how you trust Him for a supernatural turnaround! Thank Him for the miracle!

Today I decree that discouragement turns into encouragement, setbacks become increase, fear becomes faith, and all lack turns into surplus.

CHALLENGING PLACES EASED

DECREE

Today we decree that the challenging places in your life become easier. We call upon the God who makes the crooked places straight and the rough places plain. We command every opposing mountain and hindrance to be removed in the Name of Jesus! We pray for God's guidance and assurance as you take the next steps before you and that you shall be surefooted as you go. We pray that you have a divine ability from God to make wise decisions with confidence. We pray for strength, energy, and renewed faith. May the Spirit of the Lord cause you to experience relief from that which has been difficult and hard to navigate and may you come into a season of rest! We decree this to be so in Jesus' mighty Name!

SCRIPTURE

Every valley shall be exalted, and every mountain and hill shall be made low: and the crooked shall be made straight, and the rough places plain (Isaiah 40:4).

JOURNAL

Draw a crooked path and label it with a difficulty you are facing in life. Then draw a straight path (get a ruler if you need one!) and write that problem again—but this time also write down a Scripture you are standing on to help you overcome it!

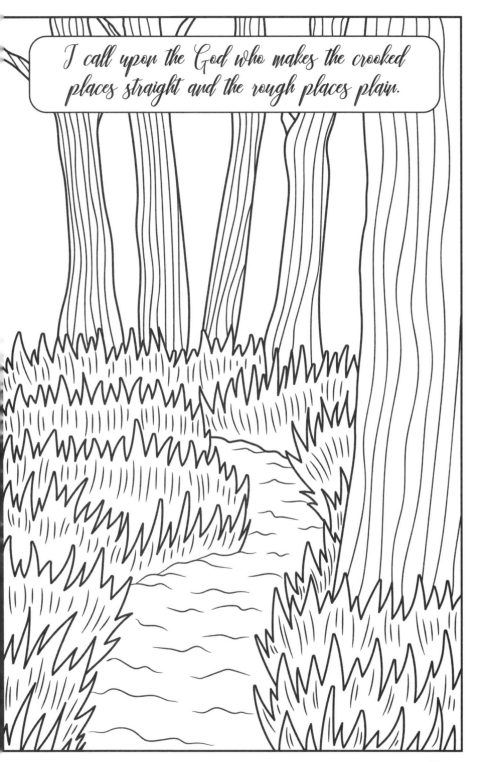

Fresh Inspiration and Vision

Decree

Today we decree that lost vision and purpose are restored. We pray that you receive refreshed inspiration concerning every project before you and for your future. May you see your God-given destiny with a renewed mindset. We declare that you become motivated to accomplish everything God has called you to do. We bind up the power of discouragement, lethargy, and indifference in Jesus' Name! We break every pattern and repetitive cycle of failure and say it will not continue. We speak new life to everything that has grown stale and fallen dormant. We decree your gifts and talents are stirred up afresh. We call for a supernatural wave of enthusiasm, passion, and determination to finish everything you have inside your heart from the Lord! You are called, anointed, and appointed for something amazing— for such a time as this!

Scripture

For the vision is yet for an appointed time, but at the end it shall speak, and not lie: though it tarry, wait for it; because it will surely come, it will not tarry (Habakkuk 2:3).

Journal

Ask God to remind you of a dream or vision you have lost and forgotten about; write it down, along with one step He shows you that you can take toward living out this dream with Him.

_____

_____

_____

_____

_____

_____

_____

I am called, anointed, and appointed for something amazing—for such a time as this!

UNEXPECTED BLESSINGS AND SURPRISES!

DECREE

Today we decree that you receive unexpected blessings, surprises, increases, and overflow. We prophesy that you shall be pleasantly surprised by good news and good reports. We declare that bad and unexpected news shall not interfere and disrupt your peace in Jesus' Name. We pray that good tidings shall break out on your right and left and it shall be as cool water that replenishes the dry places in your life. May you be divinely surprised by blessings you didn't even ask for, and we decree that good news begins to overtake all negative reports. We pray the Lord will send people in your path from many places who shall have something good to tell you. We say that you have all sufficiency in all things and your cup runs over. We pray that you will flourish abundantly and goodness and mercy will follow you wherever you go in Jesus' mighty Name!

SCRIPTURE

Finally hearing good news from a distant land is like a drink of cold water when you are dry and thirsty (Proverbs 25:25 GNT).

JOURNAL

Journal a time when a completely unexpected blessing arrived in your life. Ask God for a new surprise today!

I will flourish abundantly and goodness and mercy will follow me wherever I go in Jesus' mighty Name!

NO WEAPON OF LIES CAN PROSPER!

DECREE

We decree today that no weapon formed against you can prevail. Every weapon of wrongful accusation or indictment must bow to the Name of Jesus. Today, we declare you are able to put on the full armor of God that you may stand firm against the works of the evil one and rise above every word of judgement. We say any word or rumor unjustly uttered against you shall crumble and fail. We bind up every demonic assault against your character in Jesus' Name. You will not be overcome by losses, decreases, or setbacks from things said that are not true. We declare that every lie perpetrated by the forces of darkness is exposed and silenced. May your mind be clear from the enemy's whispers. We declare that your victory and freedom manifests speedily in Jesus' Name!

SCRIPTURE

No weapon that is formed against thee shall prosper; and every tongue that shall rise against thee in judgment thou shalt condemn. This is the heritage of the servants of the Lord, and their righteousness is of me, saith the Lord (Isaiah 54:17).

JOURNAL

Ask the Holy Spirit to reveal to you any lies of the enemy you may have believed. Write them down and next to them write down the truth that is opposite the enemy's lies!

_____

_____

_____

_____

_____

_____

_____

I decree today that no weapon formed against me can prevail.

Strength to Forgive

Decree

Today we declare that you receive the strength and ability to forgive every person who has hurt, betrayed, mistreated, and wronged you. May the overwhelming power of God's forgiveness rise up within. We decree that every painful memory is erased from your soul. May the burden of every offense and transgression committed against you be released from your shoulders. We prophesy that you are liberated from the stronghold of unforgiveness that would interfere with your prayers and rob your peace. We say that you are able to set aside the misdeeds of others and move forward into your bright future. We speak this and say you are able to freely say, "I forgive them in Jesus' Name!"

Scripture

And when ye stand praying, forgive, if ye have ought against any: that your Father also which is in heaven may forgive you your trespasses (Mark 11:25).

Journal

Who do you need to forgive today? Write their names and release them to God.

_____

_____

_____

_____

_____

_____

_____

_____

_____

_____

Today I declare that I receive the strength and ability to forgive every person who has hurt, betrayed, mistreated, and wronged me.

A KEEN EAR TO HEAR

DECREE

We decree that you have a keen ear to hear the voice, instruction, mind, and direction of the Holy Spirit. We say that you are able to know what the Spirit is saying in this important hour. We declare you carry an understanding of what heaven is doing and you know the times and seasons of God. We prophesy that you will never be confused or pulled off course by the man-made trends of the current culture. We break the power of confusion, manipulation, and peer pressure that would come to dissuade you from the call and purposes of the Holy Spirit. May you have a sharpened ear to know when the Spirit would interrupt your plans and intentions. We say that you are one who can interpret the strategies of God. We prophesy that you can hear the wind of the spirit and know which way to follow in Jesus' Name.

SCRIPTURE

If any man have ears to hear, let him hear (Mark 4:23).

JOURNAL

Journal what you hear God speak to you today. Then press in and ask Him to speak again, and write that down too!

I declare I carry an understanding of what heaven is doing and I know the times and seasons of God.

JOY AND LAUGHTER

DECREE

Today we decree you receive joy unspeakable and full of glory! May laughter fill your heart and a smile flood your countenance. We take authority over every stronghold of grief, sorrow, depression, hopelessness, and anguish. We command every dark cloud over you to dissipate in the Name of Jesus. We declare your thoughts become filled with the light of God's goodness. We pray you receive a fresh sense of hope, confidence, faith, and purpose regarding your future. We prophesy that you experience gladness in your heart. We pray that you rise up in renewed faith that enables you to see that *everything* is going to be alright! We are asking God that you will receive good news today! Declare it's going to be a great day!

SCRIPTURE

A merry heart doeth good like a medicine: but a broken spirit drieth the bones (Proverbs 17:22).

JOURNAL

Practice laughter today! Ask the Holy Spirit to reveal something humorous to you right now. Write it down and begin to laugh!

A DEEP CLEANSING

DECREE

Today we declare that you shall experience a fresh cleansing from the Spirit of God. We prophesy a deep cleaning that clears your mind, changes your ideas, invades your heart, and draws you closer to the Lord. May the fuller's soap of heaven wash your life from all levels of contamination that would place a wedge between you and the Holy One. We decree right now a washing of the water of God's Word to clear from you all the debris of this world. May you be flooded with clean spiritual water and goes into the depths of your soul in Jesus' Name. We undo all the powers of the enemy that would contaminate, infiltrate, and degrade your spiritual purity and solidarity. Right now we speak that you are clean, renewed, and purified by the fire and power of the precious Holy Spirit!

SCRIPTURE

But who may abide the day of his coming? and who shall stand when he appeareth? for he is like a refiner's fire, and like fullers' soap (Malachi 3:2).

JOURNAL

Write a prayer asking God to come in and clean every part of your mind—including places you are not aware need cleaning. Journal anything He specifically addresses.

I am flooded with clean spiritual water that goes into the depths of my soul in Jesus' Name.

IMMEASURABLE PEACE

DECREE

Today we decree you receive immeasurable peace. We declare that you are surrounded by both external and internal peace that passes understanding and overrides thoughts of fear, doubt, worry, and anxiety. We speak to every area of nervousness and say that it is dissipated by the supernatural peace of God in Jesus' Name. We bind every storm that is trying to create chaos and steal your peace and we declare to those storms, "Peace, be still!" May your mind, will, and emotions come into soundness and wholeness regarding every circumstance in your life. We declare that your heart is filled with faith and assurance and we say that you will reach the other side of every difficult journey and you shall do so in victory! We decree it in Jesus' glorious Name!

SCRIPTURE

Be careful for nothing; but in every thing by prayer and supplication with thanksgiving let your requests be made known unto God. And the peace of God, which passeth all understanding, shall keep your hearts and minds through Christ Jesus (Philippians 4:6-7).

JOURNAL

What is an area of your life that is troubling and hard to find peace in? Write it down and invite the Lord into this place.

_____

_____

_____

_____

_____

_____

I am surrounded by both external and internal peace that passes understanding and overrides thoughts of fear, doubt, worry, and anxiety.

ANOTHER LEVEL OF GROWTH

DECREE

Today we declare that you grow and graduate to another level in the spirit. We say that you come into a new degree of spiritual maturity, ability, and understanding. We command every hindering spirit that would come to stunt your growth to be bound in Jesus' Name. We prophesy that you rise from all previous distractions and interruptions and that all areas of spiritual immaturity are replaced by wisdom and readiness. We decree another level of promotion comes upon you to elevate you to new places of influence and leadership. We call for every platform that God has designed you to stand upon to manifest in the right timing and nothing shall interfere with it. We say another level of growth develops and comes into full fruition!

SCRIPTURE

Till we all come in the unity of the faith, and of the knowledge of the Son of God, unto a perfect man, unto the measure of the stature of the fulness of Christ: that we henceforth be no more children, tossed to and fro, and carried about with every wind of doctrine, by the sleight of men, and cunning craftiness, whereby they lie in wait to deceive (Ephesians 4:13-14).

JOURNAL

List some areas in your life where you are needing to grow so you can experience promotion. Then make a second list of the promotions you expect to see as a result of your personal growth!

Today I declare that I grow and graduate to another level in the spirit.

MOUNTAINS REMOVED!

DECREE

Today we speak to obstacles, mountains, and hindrances and command them to be removed in Jesus' Name. We declare that nothing can stand in the way of answers to prayer, miracles, and breakthroughs. We prophesy to the destroying mountains and say, "The Lord is against you!" We command the high places and strongholds of the enemy to come down from around all that concerns you. We say they shall be entirely moved out of your way, never to be resurrected again. We say every mountain that stands against you shall be brought low and become a plain, and you will not continue to circle the same old mountains and obstacles again. Mountains shall melt like wax at the presence of the Lord that is upon you. We declare you are going over and not going under, for the mountains have been removed!

SCRIPTURE

Who art thou, O great mountain? before Zerubbabel thou shalt become a plain: and he shall bring forth the headstone thereof with shoutings, crying, Grace, grace unto it (Zechariah 4:7).

JOURNAL

Draw a mountain and label it with an obstacle you are facing. Now draw that mountain leveled flat under the Name of Jesus!

_____

_____

_____

_____

_____

_____

_____

_____

Today I speak to obstacles, mountains, and hindrances and command them to be removed in Jesus' Name.

FINANCIAL PROVISION COMES NOW!

Decree

We decree you begin receiving divine and unexpected financial provision to meet every need. We say that debts and deficits are removed and bills are paid on time, every time. We speak that there is financial peace in your life and what has been lacking begins to be filled and supplied. We declare that increase begins to surround your life long term and we declare a settling of all financial problems and issues. We say you receive gainful employment and stable incomes for your work. In Jesus' Name we bind the enemy's power from creating excess breakdowns and repairs creating excess expenses that rob your resources. We declare financial provision comes now!

Scripture

But my God shall supply all your need according to his riches in glory by Christ Jesus (Philippians 4:19).

Journal

Write down a time when God supernaturally supplied a financial need. Write Him a thank-you note, then trust Him to do it again!

I declare financial provision comes now!

ANGELS DESCENDING AND SURROUNDING

DECREE

Today we call upon the Lord God of Hosts to commission the reinforcements of His mighty angels to surround your life, your home, family, property, and business. We thank God, according to His promise, that angels have been commissioned to bear you up in their hands so that you will not experience injury, accident, tragedy, or calamity. We call for the angels to protect against all attack, violence, burglary, break-in, mischief, and mayhem. As we speak God's Word, we call for angels to descend and work as ministering servants for us who are heirs of salvation. May angels surround each of your loved ones that they may be safe from all harm and injury. Today we declare in full assurance that angels are standing watch as you sleep and cover you from before and behind. We declare the angels of the Lord are working for you and are on your side!

SCRIPTURE

For he shall give his angels charge over thee, to keep thee in all thy ways. They shall bear thee up in their hands, lest thou dash thy foot against a stone (Psalm 91:11-12).

JOURNAL

Write an invitation requesting that God send angels into your life to attend to a situation.

I call for angels to descend and work as ministering servants for me—an heir of salvation.

Your Fruitful Season Begins Now

Decree

Today we decree that everything that has been locked up and shut up by the enemy is loosed! We declare your days of wilderness and desert living are over! We say you are coming out of every demonic prison constructed unjustly and illegally by the enemy. Every mental block, mind-binding spirit, and every spiritual and physical restriction is broken in the Name of Jesus! We call you loosed from every oppression and we say you are spiritually, emotionally, and physically free! We declare you are loosed to live and breathe and operate in all the fullness and plan of God on every level designed for you. You are like a planted tree that bears fruit against the current of a flowing river. We say *your season of fruitfulness begins now!*

Scripture

And he shall be like a tree planted by the rivers of water, that bringeth forth his fruit in his season; his leaf also shall not wither; and whatsoever he doeth shall prosper (Psalm 1:3).

Journal

What area of your life do you see the most fruit in? Write down your thanks to God for it. Now journal the area in which you see the least fruit, and thank God for the fruit He is about to create here.

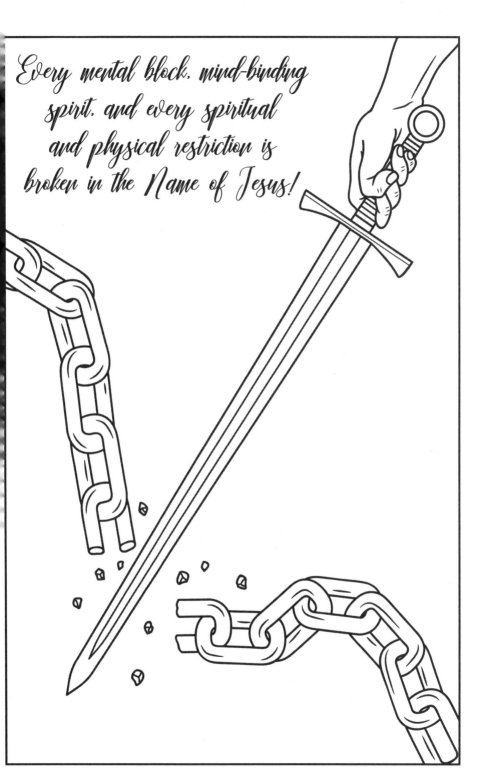

Every mental block, mind-binding spirit, and every spiritual and physical restriction is broken in the Name of Jesus!

OVERWHELMING LOVE OF THE FATHER

DECREE

Today we decree that, as a child of God, you experience the overwhelming love of the Father. May you sense His care that covers each of your needs and that you are safe under the shadow of His wings. We bind all feelings of insecurity, abandonment, and rejection in Jesus' Name. May you receive from God a genuine revelation of fatherly love. We pray that the sure arm of God's strength and stability would keep you in complete confidence that He will never leave or forsake you. May your faith be strengthened knowing that He is listening when you call and is quick to answer you when you cry, "Abba, Father!" Yes, you are a child of God and *all* shall be well with you!

SCRIPTURE

For ye have not received the spirit of bondage again to fear; but ye have received the Spirit of adoption, whereby we cry, Abba, Father. The Spirit itself beareth witness with our spirit, that we are the children of God (Romans 8:15-16).

JOURNAL

Write a letter to your Heavenly Father expressing your love for Him. Include these words in the letter: "I love you Abba Father!"

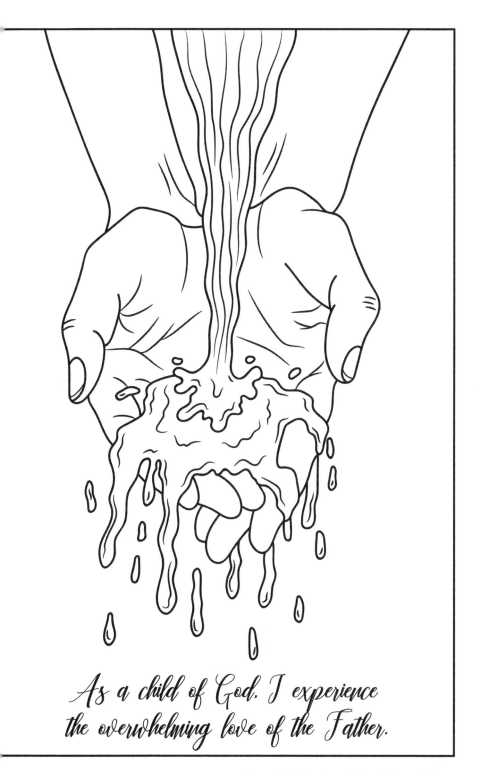

As a child of God, I experience
the overwhelming love of the Father.

RELATIONSHIPS HEALED AND RESTORED

DECREE

We decree that every strained relationship that is not meant to be in your life begins to experience divine healing and restoration. We take authority over the demonic powers of strife, division, anger, and misunderstanding in the Name of Jesus. We declare a disruption and severance from all outside interference and influence that is not from God. May hearts and minds begin to see things from a clearer heavenly perspective. We speak that each person's eyes shall be opened to reason and shall strive for peace. We say that the truth of the Holy Spirit begins to reign upon and change everything that is out of order. We pray that each person involved will turn to God and not rely on the arm of flesh. We decree unity, oneness of mind, love, understanding, forgiveness, grace, and peace. We say that your relationships are healed and restored in Jesus' Name!

SCRIPTURE

Make every effort to keep yourselves united in the Spirit, binding yourselves together with peace (Ephesians 4:3 NLT).

JOURNAL

Write the name of one person with whom you have a strained relationship, which you feel the Holy Spirit wants to repair. Write your name across from theirs, then connect your names by drawing a cross with Jesus' Name, and thank God for full restoration!

I say that my relationships
are healed and restored
in Jesus' Name!

VISIONS AND DREAMS FROM GOD

DECREE

We decree that you are positioned to receive divine dreams and visions of God as He desires to bring them upon you. We say that any blockage, hindrance, and demonic interference cannot disrupt your receptivity to heaven's impartation. We call today for the last-days manifestation of dreams and visions to rest upon your life so that you begin to hear from the Spirit in a supernatural way. We declare you have the precise ability to separate natural dreams from spiritual ones. We say that you possess the ability to see and hear accurately into the spirit realm in alignment with the Holy Spirit. May you have dreams of inspiration that give you new ideas, concepts, and thoughts. We call for clear vision and divine imaginations to work within you that shall enable you to accomplish great things. We ask God to allow you to dream dreams and see visions that are given by heaven for this season in Jesus' Name!

SCRIPTURE

And it shall come to pass in the last days, saith God, I will pour out of my Spirit upon all flesh: and your sons and your daughters shall prophesy, and your young men shall see visions, and your old men shall dream dreams: and on my servants and on my handmaidens I will pour out in those days of my Spirit; and they shall prophesy (Acts 2:17-18).

JOURNAL

Journal a dream! If you can't remember one, ask God to speak to you tonight as you sleep, and journal your dream tomorrow morning, first thing, before you forget it.

_____

_____

_____

_____

_____

I decree that I am positioned to receive divine dreams and visions of God.

RESTFUL SLEEP

DECREE

We decree that you begin to experience restful sleep like never before. In Jesus' Name, we break the power of restlessness, sleeplessness, insomnia, tensions, and physical distress that would rob you of a good night's rest. We cast out every nightmare and night terror and we say it cannot operate ever again around you or your home! We speak peace to your mind and body during the night hours. We say that every muscle, bone, cell, organ, and hormone must align itself correctly so you are able to rest. We speak peace to the environment around you and say that you operate in God's promise that He gives His beloved sleep. We speak sweet sleep upon you and may your nights be restful, comfortable, relaxing, and calm. We say that your nights of sleep shall be the best and most rejuvenating yet! Amen!

SCRIPTURE

It is vain for you to rise up early, to sit up late, to eat the bread of sorrows: for so he giveth his beloved sleep (Psalm 127:2).

JOURNAL

Journal one thing you will do today to prepare yourself for a good night's sleep. (The internet has lots of suggestions; pick a relevant one.) Commit to doing your part and trust God to bless your rest above and beyond expectations.

I say that my nights of sleep shall be the best and most rejuvenating yet! Amen!

OPEN DOORS AND DIVINE APPOINTMENTS

DECREE

We decree open doors of opportunity, utterance, and divine appointments from heaven come your way. May you be positioned to walk into the right places and situations that set you up for success and influence. We declare that closed doors of rejection shall not be your experience and the only doors that close are those God has closed. We say the enemy has no ability to create blockage and barriers to the places you are destined by God to enter. We declare you receive heavenly appointed phone calls, letters, contacts, contracts, meetings, assignments, platforms, and engagements. We decree that you are given divine opportunities to speak the Word of God and further the Gospel. We call for doors of influence that you didn't even expect and we declare today that a new day of open doors rests upon you!

SCRIPTURE

For a great door and effectual is opened unto me, and there are many adversaries (1 Corinthians 16:9).

JOURNAL

Make a list of where you will go and what you will do today, and surrender this list to Jesus, asking Him to open doors for you throughout your day.

I am given divine opportunities to speak the Word of God and further the Gospel.

ENCOUNTERS WITH HIS GLORY

DECREE

Today we declare that you begin to encounter a new level of God's weight and glory. May you experience the power of His might and majesty on a level that causes you to fall on your knees in humble worship. We say that you supernaturally see His beauty, perfection, depth, and strength. We decree you have a divine revelation of how limitless He is. We declare that you will intimately know the God who created all things, for by Him all things consist and are being upheld by the word of His power. May His goodness pass before you that you will know with certainty that His presence is going with you wherever you go. We prophesy that you will sense His majestic strength in your home, workplace, and community and live and function as a carrier of His great glory. We say that the glory of the Lord will shine all about you and emanate from within you. We prophesy this day that you shall enter into new realms and encounters with His glory, in Jesus' Name!

SCRIPTURE

And the glory which thou gavest me I have given them (John 17:22).

JOURNAL

Make another list like yesterday; keep your eyes open to spot God's glory in each place or task. Add them to your list later, and as you review this list, praise God for revealing Himself in every part of your life.

I will sense His majestic strength in my home, workplace, and community and live and function as a carrier of His great glory.

SATISFIED WITH LONG, ABUNDANT LIFE

DECREE

We decree that you shall live a long life and shall live to a full age. We declare nothing shall be able to cut your life short. We break the power of early and premature death over you and your loved ones in the Name of Jesus. We say no evil shall be able to end your life before your fullness of days is fulfilled. We prophesy that you live long and strong with days full of strength and vitality. We prophesy that your quality of life is enhanced and that you are filled with physical vigor and stamina. We speak to your whole person—spirit, soul, and body—and say that you are purpose-driven, active, and functioning to your fullest potential. May the God of life move through your entire being so that you shall experience the divine and supernatural life that comes from the Lord. We declare you shall experience as many sunrises and sunsets as your heart desires. We say this day that you shall be satisfied with a long and abundant life!

SCRIPTURE

With long life will I satisfy him, and shew him my salvation (Psalm 91:16).

JOURNAL

Ask the Holy Spirit to show you a picture of yourself flourishing and excelling in old age. Write down a list of things you expect to see yourself experiencing during those premiere years of your life (for example, your grandkids college graduations or them getting married etc).

I say this day
that I shall be
satisfied with a long
and abundant life!

NEW REALMS OF PRAYER

DECREE

We decree that your prayer life elevates to another level and that you begin to navigate new realms with God. We prophesy that rivers of living water begin to flood from your innermost being. May you enter into the deeper places of communion and fellowship with the Father, Son, and Holy Spirit. We prophesy a new confidence of faith in the things you pray that assures you they shall be answered. We speak a new unlocking in your prayer language that brings about new heavenly dialects as you speak and sing with the tongues of men and of angels. May you pray in unison and cohesion with the Spirit of God, and we decree a new outflow begins to come forth. We break the power of the enemy from trying to disrupt your prayer time and bring unnecessary distractions. We say that your time of prayer shall be sweet, fulfilling, and productive and that you are entering a new level in prayer!

SCRIPTURE

He that believeth on me, as the scripture hath said, out of his belly shall flow rivers of living water (John 7:38).

JOURNAL

Journal together with the Holy Spirit's help the areas where your prayer life needs to advance to new levels. For example, to experience His voice more clearly, be less distracted, develop greater intimacy with the Father or enter new realms while praying in the Spirit.

I say that my time of prayer shall be sweet, fulfilling, and productive and I am entering a new level in prayer!

SET APART AS A HOLY VESSEL

DECREE

Today we decree that you are set apart as a holy vessel for the work and purposes of God. We prophesy that you live as a chosen generation, royal priesthood, and holy nation called to manifest His praises. We say you are purged from all contaminants and you are sanctified and separated for the Master's use. We speak that you shall function in the purpose and position God has ordained for you and shall not be sidetracked or inhibited in Jesus' Name. We bind every generational curse from infiltrating your destiny and you shall be found worthy for your divine occupation. We declare you are a vessel that is being beautifully prepared for every Kingdom task and that you have insight into the hope of your heavenly calling and inheritance. We decree you are a holy servant and a refined vessel fully prepared for the work of the Lord!

SCRIPTURE

But in a great house there are not only vessels of gold and of silver, but also of wood and of earth; and some to honour, and some to dishonour. If a man therefore purge himself from these, he shall be a vessel unto honour, sanctified, and meet for the master's use, and prepared unto every good work (2 Timothy 2:20-21).

JOURNAL

Ask the Holy Spirit to reveal any areas that may be keeping you from walking as a holy vessel before the Lord. Then write some things you need to do make changes in these areas.

_____

_____

_____

_____

_____

Today I decree that I am set apart as a holy vessel for the work and purposes of God.

DIVINE HEALTH RESTS UPON YOU

DECREE

We decree that you experience divine health, healing, and wholeness. We take authority over the curse of sickness, disease, viruses, pain, and suffering in Jesus' Name. We command every adverse physical and chronic condition to leave your body and all spirits of infirmity must depart from you. We speak upon you the divine healing promise that Jesus took your sickness and carried your diseases. We say that all meddling ailments, syndromes, disorders, irritations, aches, and discomforts must cease and desist. We speak to your body now and command it to align itself and function the way it was created. We decree you are alleviated from everything that would make you susceptible to disease. We speak and say that your immune system is miraculously strengthened and your health springs forth speedily. We declare it manifests *now* in Jesus' Name!

SCRIPTURE

When the even was come, they brought unto him many that were possessed with devils: and he cast out the spirits with his word, and healed all that were sick: that it might be fulfilled which was spoken by Esaias the prophet, saying, Himself took our infirmities, and bare our sicknesses (Matthew 8:16-17).

JOURNAL

Draw a cross, and write on it the name of every ailment that you have had or that you worry about. Thank Jesus for taking your infirmities and giving you divine health!

I speak upon myself
the divine healing promise
that Jesus took my sickness
and carried my diseases.

A FRESH CONFIDENCE

DECREE

We decree right now that you receive a new measure of confidence and courage. We speak that that you live and operate in certainty and assurance about who God has made you. May there be a new morale that comes over your heart and mind. In the Name of Jesus, we break the powers of rejection, shyness, and insecurity from having a voice in your thoughts. May you see yourself in a new light as one who is poised, able, and capable. We say you will not have any hesitation to stand before any person or audience that you are positioned to address. We prophesy that you walk into every circumstance and situation with assurance knowing that you are secure because the Greater One lives within you! We decree no fear and that you are confident in Him!

SCRIPTURE

For the Lord shall be thy confidence, and shall keep thy foot from being taken (Proverbs 3:26).

JOURNAL

When do you feel most insecure? Write how you would feel in those situations if you could see the Lord Jesus walking alongside you. What would you say and do differently knowing He is next to you?

I walk into every circumstance and situation with assurance knowing that I am secure because the Greater One lives within me!

MANIFESTING SIGNS AND WONDERS!

DECREE

We declare that you are one who carries the miraculous upon you and that you operate in the supernatural manifestations of God for this generation. We say that heavenly signs confirm the word that flows from your mouth. We decree that every hindrance and blockage that would prevent the supernatural breaks now in Jesus' Name. We take authority over every man-made ideology and empty religious tradition that would keep the mighty works of God from being displayed. We say that you come to know the supernatural attributes of God that enable you to speak with new tongues, cast out demons, and lay hands upon the sick. May you operate in the miraculous power of the Spirit without restraint whenever the need arises. We say signs, wonders, and miracles follow you in Jesus' Name!

SCRIPTURE

Behold, I and the children whom the Lord hath given me are for signs and for wonders (Isaiah 8:18).

JOURNAL

What is one miracle you have seen God do through someone else? Write down a plan to step out in the same way, trusting Him to use you just like He uses others.

_____

_____

_____

_____

_____

_____

_____

_____

I boldly say that I shall
endure all hard situations
and come out in total victory!

A SONG IN YOUR HEART

DECREE

We decree that your heart is filled with song. May you well up with rejoicing, celebration, joy, and singing. May you become overjoyed for the marvelous things the Lord has done. We break the power of all sadness and gloominess that would steal the song in your heart. We say that every spirit of defeat is bound and not allowed to fill your mind in Jesus' Name. May the song in your heart overtake all negative emotions and give you a renewed sense of confident victory. We prophesy that you receive new songs inspired by the Holy Spirit that declare the wonderful works of God in your life. We declare you receive new revelation through song. We decree songs, new songs, hymns, spiritual songs, and melodies come forth from within you, all to the glory and praise of the Lord. May the song of the Lord well up within you today!

SCRIPTURE

Oh, sing to the Lord a new song, for He has done marvelous deeds! His right hand and His holy arm have accomplished deliverance (Psalm 98:1 MEV).

JOURNAL

Write your song! If the song welling up in your heart happens to be written by someone else, journal the lyrics that speak for you today.

I well up
with rejoicing,
celebration, joy,
and singing.

Safe Travel and Transit

Decree

We decree that you are safe in all manner of travel, transport, and transit. May every vehicle or any method you use to commute be safe and delivered from breakdown or accident. We prophesy that when you walk your foot shall not stumble or fall. You are safe when you come in and when you go out. We call for the angelic hosts to come and protect you from all harm. In Jesus' Name, we declare that all spirits of harassment, hindrance, tragedy, or calamity are forbidden to operate against you when you travel or commute. We say the angels will hold every vehicle or method of transport in their hands. We declare that you will always reach your intended destinations safely and in peace. We say your paths and routes are always divinely guided by the hand of the Lord. We decree that all travel is safe and secure in Jesus' Name!

Scripture

Blessed shalt thou be when thou comest in, and blessed shalt thou be when thou goest out (Deuteronomy 28:6).

Journal

What is your next trip, when, and where? Write down the details of the journey and place them under God's divine protection right now.

_____

_____

_____

_____

_____

_____

I say my paths and routes are always divinely guided by the hand of the Lord.

A SWORD IN YOUR MOUTH!

DECREE

We decree the sword of the Lord is in your mouth. May the things you speak be filled with divine truth and heavenly revelation. We prophesy that your words carry power to bless, heal, deliver, and exhort. May you be anointed to speak with taste and grace, class and poise. We declare you receive confidence when you open your mouth that you always know what to say and how to share it. We pray that the Lord places a watch over your lips to prevent you from speaking anything contrary to what is right and godly. We decree that your words shall be a polished weapon against the forces of darkness. We prophesy that your words are filled with heavenly authority and capture the attention of your hearers. May you know when to speak and when to refrain from speaking, and we say an anointing comes upon your speech enabling you to speak a right word in due season as the sword of heaven comes from your mouth!

SCRIPTURE

And he hath made my mouth like a sharp sword; in the shadow of his hand hath he hid me, and made me a polished shaft; in his quiver hath he hid me (Isaiah 49:2).

JOURNAL

After asking the Lord to put His word in your mouth, journal what He gives you. Ask Him to show you when and where to share or speak that word!

_____

_____

_____

_____

_____

_____

_____

I decree that my words shall be a polished weapon against the forces of darkness.

TRUSTED FRIENDSHIPS

DECREE

We declare that you begin to experience godly and trusted friendships. We say that every acquaintance or relationship that enters your life that is not from God is interrupted and disrupted in the Name of Jesus. We break the enemy's power from planting any person in your life who has a wrong agenda or toxic behaviors. In Jesus' Name we break the powers of witchcraft from inserting the wrong people in your life. We break the powers of abandonment, guilt, betrayal, and alienation from your soul. We prophesy that you possess within you the ability to trust others. We decree that you will always enjoy friendships with godly people who are trustworthy and reliable. May the Lord send the right people into your life so that you are surrounded by wholesome relationships that edify. We decree you shall not live in loneliness and shall not ever feel that you don't have supportive friends around you in your times of need. We say that your life is filled with trusted friendships!

SCRIPTURE

Iron sharpens iron, so a man sharpens the countenance of his friend (Proverbs 27:17 MEV).

JOURNAL

If you feel you only have a few friends, ask the Lord to show you those that you may not realize are already your friends. Then draw a few blanks indicating space for new friends that are coming!

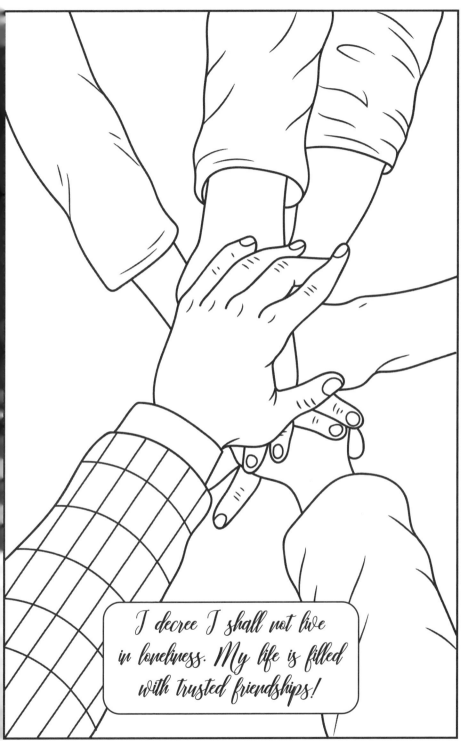

I decree I shall not live in loneliness. My life is filled with trusted friendships!

STRONG AND RESILIENT

DECREE

We declare that you receive supernatural strength to endure the pressures of this life. We prophesy you are strong, resilient, and firm. We decree you are able to withstand in the evil day without buckling. We say that you rise up in the power of God's might so that you are able to wage war successfully against principalities, powers, rulers of darkness, and spiritual wickedness in heavenly places. We command all intense stress, pressure, mayhem, and chaos to be alleviated in the Name of Jesus! We decree you will not faint or grow weary and that anxiety has no hold over you. You shall not look around you in terror or fear. We prophesy that the Spirit of the Lord will harden you to difficulty and you shall see the Lord's help upon and around you. We declare today that you bounce back from every challenge and that you stand up strong!

SCRIPTURE

Fear not [there is nothing to fear], for I am with you; do not look around you in terror and be dismayed, for I am your God. I will strengthen and harden you to difficulties, yes, I will help you; yes, I will hold you up and retain you with My [victorious] right hand of rightness and justice (Isaiah 41:10 AMPC).

JOURNAL

Journal a time when you felt unable to cope with something. Compare that situation with Jesus' strength. Thank Him for giving you that same strength to overcome!

I declare today that I bounce
back from every challenge
and that I stand up strong!

NO FEAR OF MAN

DECREE

We decree that all fear of man is broken from your life. You shall not carry a concern or any manner of anxiety of what others might say or do against you. We declare that all forms of intimidation and any sense of threat in your mind are driven from you. We prophesy that no assailant, antagonist, abuser, invader, or aggressor shall ever be able to touch you or come against you in the Name of Jesus! We speak that you are loosed from the strong arm of any person who has set themselves as an enemy and we declare, "Peace!" We decree over your mind and say that your thoughts are immersed in the help of the Lord that is around you right now preventing any evil. We decree a confidence in the Lord's defense that is working on your behalf enabling you to say, "What can man do to me?" From this day forward all fear of man is broken from your life!

SCRIPTURE

The Lord is with me; I will not be afraid. What can mere mortals do to me? (Psalm 118:6 NIV)

JOURNAL

Envision yourself in your heavenly seat of authority next to Jesus. Now write about a situation from your life on earth when fear of man or intimidation attacked you. Describe how that threat looks now, from your heavenly point of view.

_____

_____

_____

_____

_____

_____

Instruction and Intelligence

Decree

Today we decree you receive revelation and instruction from the Lord. We declare that it becomes easy for you to receive wisdom, teaching, information, and ideas. We say that every mental block or intellectual gap is broken and your mind is able to comprehend and understand. We prophesy that a brilliancy and intelligence of mind comes upon you. We decree you have the capacity to reason correctly and make good judgments. We say that your memory is blessed and that it functions at its full measure. We pray for supernatural teaching from the Lord to permeate your mind and your heart. May the Great Instructor teach you His ways regarding the important elements and situations surrounding your life that keep you steps ahead of the enemy. We break the power of any distraction that would prevent you from keeping the Lord as the center of your learning processes. We say that you function in the intelligent ability the Lord has given you and that His instruction is upon you!

Scripture

Teach me thy way, O Lord, and lead me in a plain path, because of mine enemies (Psalm 27:11).

Journal

Write down a question you don't know the answer to, asking the Lord to give you insight. Take notes on what He tells you!

_____

_____

_____

_____

_____

_____

_____

I function in the intelligent ability the Lord has given me and His instruction is upon me!

UNITY WITH THE BODY OF CHRIST

DECREE

We declare that you live in harmony and unity with your fellow believers. We prophesy that a sense of kinship resides in your spirit that enables you to maintain oneness with your brothers and sisters in Christ. May you be able to properly discern the Lord's Body in truth and love. We say the power of misunderstanding, division, miscommunication, and discord are broken and replaced by communication, understanding, and agreement. May you be able to find places of peace and harmony even with those with whom you cannot see eye to eye on certain viewpoints. May you be free from any hurts or feelings of betrayal caused by a brother or sister in the Lord. May the ability to forgive be the element that reigns supreme in your heart, and we say you experience the pleasantness that comes from being united. We decree you are able to effectively function in the local church body and supply a positive contribution to the Kingdom of God. May your unity with the Body of Christ descend like the oil of the Holy Spirit upon your life in Jesus' Name!

SCRIPTURE

Behold, how good and how pleasant it is for brethren to dwell together in unity! (Psalm 133:1)

JOURNAL

Have you experienced strain on the unity of believers around you? Journal it, and bring it under the love of Christ.

_____

_____

_____

_____

_____

I live in harmony and unity with my fellow believers.

DECLARATION FOR ISRAEL

DECREE

We decree over the nation of Israel the word, "Peace!" We speak peace, safety, and security over Israel. May every enemy set against them be disrupted and interrupted from their evil intent. May the Lord cause Israel to retain all the land that is rightfully theirs. We pray that the nations would be at peace with Israel and that they would be free from unfair political maneuvers and agreements. We prophesy a supernatural peace to come upon the citizens so that they live free from dread and fear. We say that the Gospel shall go forth in Israel unhindered and with great success and the word of God shall not return void. We pray the Lord would cause His blessing to be upon you, Israel, and may your friends, neighbors, and even your enemies see the unique and supernatural hand of God upon you. We say Israel and Jerusalem are prosperous, blessed, and safe in Jesus' Name!

SCRIPTURE

Pray for the peace of Jerusalem: they shall prosper that love thee (Psalm 122:6).

JOURNAL

Write a blessing over Israel with your own words.

_____

_____

_____

_____

_____

_____

_____

_____

_____

_____

I speak peace, safety,
and security over Israel.

PRODIGALS RETURNING

DECREE

We decree that your prodigal, backslidden, and wayward children and family members return to God. We decree that they receive revelation in the knowledge of God that brings them back into a right relationship with the Lord. We prophesy that their eyes and ears are open to truth. We break the power of every seducing, lying, and deceiving spirit in Jesus' Name. We say that any hard-heartedness, stiff-necked resistance, or rebellious spirit is broken. We command all curses of witchcraft holding them captive to be destroyed by the anointing. We declare that Gospel laborers shall be placed in their path to minister truth and life. We speak that hearts become opened and softened to the Holy Spirit. They shall return to fellowship with the Body of Christ and all relationships that would influence with evil are severed. We break every soul tie to wrong relationships, habits, and places and we declare the prodigals come home now and that a time of celebration begins!

SCRIPTURE

For this my son was dead, and is alive again; he was lost, and is found (Luke 15:24).

JOURNAL

Write the names of any prodigals in your family, church, or among your friends. After each name, label them "Saved, healed, delivered, restored to full relationship with God in Jesus' Name!"

_____

_____

_____

_____

_____

_____

I decree that my prodigal,
backslidden, and wayward children
and family members return to God.

FREE FROM THE CURSE

DECREE

We prophesy that the curse has no place or ability to function or raise its head against your life. It cannot function in your home, on your property, or in your family in the Name of Jesus. We break the power of every generational curse, iniquity, or generational sin. We say that you and your bloodline are curse free and that every curse is replaced with the generational blessing. Every element of family history that was birthed through sin and wickedness shall cease and desist and not continue to the future generations. We prophesy that going forward you shall live in the blessing and experience favor. Your mind is free from the effect of past curses and you shall no longer give time, attention, or concern to the previous curse. We decree you are curse free!

SCRIPTURE

Christ hath redeemed us from the curse of the law, being made a curse for us: for it is written, Cursed is every one that hangeth on a tree (Galatians 3:13).

JOURNAL

Journal about a past curse you faced and how Jesus set you free from it. Now write down whatever is facing you today. Thank Jesus for setting you free from this, too, but leave a blank for *how* He does it—fill that in later.

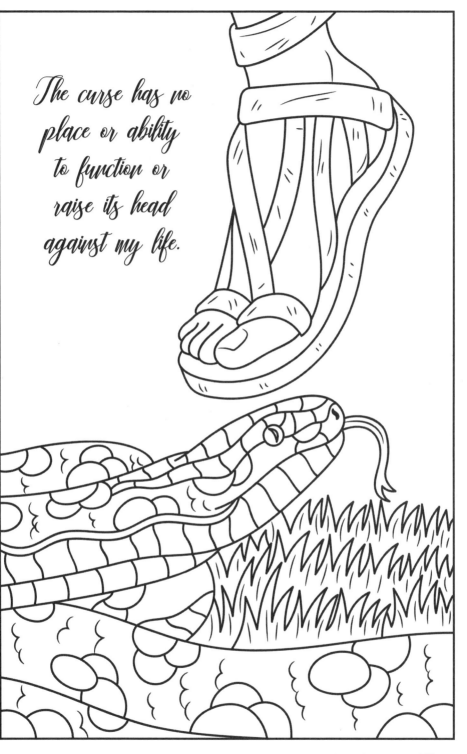

The curse has no place or ability to function or raise its head against my life.

A WELL-DESERVED BREAK!

DECREE

We decree you come into a season that is devoid of intense warfare and constant struggle. We prophesy that you experience an obvious and sudden moment of reprieve and alleviation from your battles. May you look about you in this moment and find that every enemy and attack is nowhere to be found. We declare a supernatural rest from your enemies and we speak that you enter into a well-deserved break that comes from the Lord! We speak that a season to build and progress comes upon you. Within you arises a refreshed ability to pause and enjoy life, relax, and unwind. We say that you pause to know God in a fresh new way. May your experience with the Lord become saturated with a sweet, gentle wind from the Spirit. We prophesy a calm serenity to surround you and may you return with renewed fire, zeal, and energy. We say a time to take a break and recharge comes upon you supernaturally right now!

SCRIPTURE

But now the Lord my God hath given me rest on every side, so that there is neither adversary nor evil occurrent (1 Kings 5:4).

JOURNAL

Write the Lord a note thanking Him for rest and relaxation. Commit to enjoy His gift and list ways that you will actively avoid striving and busyness during this time.

_____

_____

_____

_____

_____

_____

A time to take a break and recharge comes upon me supernaturally right now!

HIS PERFECT WILL

DECREE

We decree that the perfect will of God is being established in your life. We prophesy that you will never miss God's plan, direction, and path. We break the power of any fear that would make you anxious about making a mistake. We say of every fork in the road before you, causing you to feel uncertain about the next steps—the choice on where to go is made clear. We say you know God's perfect will concerning your family, job, finances, health, home, and calling. We declare you are sure-footed and assured of your choices and decisions as you follow God's plan. We say that your mind is renewed and you possess the ability to prove the good, acceptable, and perfect will of God. We say that you live and function in His perfect will and nothing shall be able to interfere in Jesus' Name!

SCRIPTURE

And be not conformed to this world: but be ye transformed by the renewing of your mind, that ye may prove what is that good, and acceptable, and perfect, will of God (Romans 12:2).

JOURNAL

Journal a promise you have received from the Lord that reveals His will for your life—one you have not yet seen fully realized. Step forward in the spirit today—one step closer to your destination in Him.

_____
_____
_____
_____
_____
_____
_____
_____

I decree that the perfect will of God is being established in my life.

Never Forsaken

Decree

We decree that you will never live with a feeling of being alone or forsaken. We say that whenever you face a challenge, the enemy is not able to speak lies that you are isolated and forgotten. We break the power of any feelings of abandonment, betrayal, desertion, or rejection in Jesus' Name. We prophesy that you will never live as an outcast or as lonely and will always know that you are needed and wanted. We speak that you are surrounded by the protection and care from God's loving hand. We say that you have friends and alliances that remind you that you are loved, appreciated, and deeply valued. We say that your mind carries that constant awareness that God will never leave your side and will always be with you wherever you go. We say you are never forsaken and you are always remembered and accepted in the Name of Jesus!

Scripture

Thou shalt no more be termed Forsaken; neither shall thy land any more be termed Desolate: but thou shalt be called Hephzibah, and thy land Beulah: for the Lord delighteth in thee, and thy land shall be married (Isaiah 62:4).

Journal

When in your life have you experienced a feeling of being abandoned or alone? Ask the Holy Spirit to show you how God was with you during that experience and reveal any tactics of the enemy that might still be making you feel isolated or abandoned. Write these things down.

I will never live with a feeling of being alone or forsaken.

New Identity

Decree

Today we decree that you receive and live in a new identity that is saturated in Christ. We speak that the former things that labeled you are removed and have passed away and can no longer define you. We bind the work of all previous characterizations that would tether you to the past and cause you to be seen as something that you are not. We say the former "you" is crucified and a new "you" has arisen! We sever from your memory any past images of yourself that are not in line with the image of Christ. We speak that your new identity is visible to you and all those around you. We say that your new character speaks for itself and shall bring you assurance, adulation, and acceptance. We prophesy that the new person God has made you shall show forth brightly and others shall come to the brightness upon you. We say you are a new person—the old is gone and brand new has come!

Scripture

Therefore if any man be in Christ, he is a new creature: old things are passed away; behold, all things are become new (2 Corinthians 5:17).

Journal

List old labels that used to identify you, then cross them out. Ask Jesus for one word to write down that describes your new identity in Him.

_____

_____

_____

_____

_____

_____

_____

Today I decree
that I receive
and live in a new
identity that is
saturated in Christ.

BORN TO STAND OUT

Decree

We decree you shall not live your days blending in but standing out. We say you shall shine and be promoted to represent the Kingdom. May you only experience the seasons of hiding that come from the Lord and not those that come from the enemy, who would try and keep you pushed down and held back. We decree you are being drawn out of obscurity into God's limelight of influence. We say that the unique role that you have been ordained by God to play comes to its fullest measure of effectiveness. We say you have been born for such a time and this and you shall stand out with a unique message and anointing. We say people are drawn to you and that you shall excel and emerge into an exceptional vessel of His glory and that the Name of the Lord shall be glorified in you and through you. You are born to stand out!

Scripture

Even for this same purpose have I raised thee up, that I might shew my power in thee, and that my name might be declared throughout the earth (Romans 9:17).

Journal

What is one thing that is wonderfully different about you that makes you unique and priceless in God's Kingdom?

I shall not live my days blending in but standing out.

TIME FOR A PRAISE BREAK!

DECREE

We decree that you find continual reasons to pause and give God a shout of praise. We say you see past every element of opposition and find a place of praise. May there be a shout in your mouth, rejoicing in your heart, dancing in your feet, and a clap in your hands. We decree you are quick to fall on your knees in worship. We say you are released into mighty and crazy praise. We declare nothing can steal your praise; no demon or evil spirit can steal your praise. No person or circumstance can rob your praise. We prophesy that you are impacted by sudden and overwhelming praises that well up from within. We speak that you are given to pause from what you are doing and take a moment to praise. We declare you see all the reasons around you that spark your praise. We say that you shall see the glorious greatness of your God in every situation and you will be overcome to pause and take a praise break!

SCRIPTURE

Great is the Lord and most worthy of praise; his greatness no one can fathom (Psalm 145:3 NIV).

JOURNAL

Write your praises to Jesus today!

I am impacted by sudden and overwhelming praises that well up from within.

LIFE MORE ABUNDANT

DECREE

We decree that you live a life filled with abundance. We say your quality of life improves and excels. May the abundant life of the Lord Jesus surround you. We declare that no evil spirit of lack or depletion can interrupt the abundance and sufficiency God has supplied for you. Every thief that would come to steal, kill, or destroy is bound in the Name of Jesus! We prophesy that insufficiency is turned into plenty. We declare you live with nothing missing and nothing broken. We say you live abundantly spiritually, physically, and emotionally. We say you have financial sufficiency and are bountiful in goods. May the joy and fun of living your life rest wholly upon you. We speak that you are able to do all the wonderful things that you desire and be able to do so with strength and stamina. We declare that you have all sufficiency in all things and God's grace for plentiful living abounds toward you!

SCRIPTURE

The thief cometh not, but for to steal, and to kill, and to destroy: I am come that they might have life, and that they might have it more abundantly (John 10:10).

JOURNAL

Name something that the enemy has taken from you in the past. Write a notice that you are reclaiming that by the power of Jesus' blood!

_____

_____

_____

_____

_____

_____

I prophesy that insufficiency is turned into plenty.

NO MORE SHAME

DECREE

We decree that the shame and reproach of your youth is driven from you in the Name of Jesus. We say that all manner of shame from a past season is broken off your life. May your years of youthful foolishness and immaturity be forgotten and replaced by a new season of prudence and wisdom. We say you come into your full age of maturity in the spirit. May those around you see the thoughtfulness and sensibility that rests upon you in this new season. We speak that an anointing comes upon you to provide wisdom and admonishment to others in their personal journey of growth. We speak that people, places, and circumstances shall not bring you into the condemnation of a former season of immaturity. May nothing remind you of what used to be and may you only think of where God is bringing you. We prophesy that the shame of your youth is broken and shall never return to you again!

SCRIPTURE

Fear not; for thou shalt not be ashamed: neither be thou confounded; for thou shalt not be put to shame: for thou shalt forget the shame of thy youth, and shalt not remember the reproach of thy widowhood any more (Isaiah 54:4).

JOURNAL

Is there any shame in your life? Write it down, then cross it out forever! Ask Jesus to give you a new name to write down in place of that mark of shame.

_____

_____

_____

_____

_____

HIS BODY AND BLOOD

DECREE

We decree you receive a new understanding and revelation of the Body and Blood of Christ. May the understanding of the communion meal be increased within you. We say each time you receive of the Body and Blood of our Lord in His supper that your inner being is saturated with the supernatural power that is provided in this meal. We say it causes healing, and as you receive and we declare all poisons and toxins are driven from your mind and your body. We say you are washed afresh with the cleansing blood of Jesus. May you have a clear ability to receive the supper of the Lord and be able to correctly examine yourself and also discern the Lord's Body according to the Word of God. May the communion meal become real to you and cause you to receive a revelation of the Lord Jesus and His death and resurrection in a life-changing way. We prophesy that all the benefits provided in the meal of the Lord rest upon you, within you, and around you in Jesus' Name.

SCRIPTURE

And when he had given thanks, he brake it, and said, Take, eat: this is my body, which is broken for you: this do in remembrance of me (1 Corinthians 11:24).

JOURNAL

How often do you currently take communion? Write it down, and if it doesn't seem often enough, ask the Lord to reveal additional times when it would be beneficial to receive it. How often do you think you should receive communion?

I have a clear ability to receive the supper of the Lord and correctly discern the Lord's Body.

THE LIVING WORD OF GOD

DECREE

We decree today that the living Word of God dwells in you richly with all wisdom and truth. We say that you are removed from the vain philosophies of the day and that you are clothed with the Word of Truth found in the Scriptures. We say you are drawn to give your full attention to His Word and that you meditate upon it in your heart and mind. We say your ear is inclined to hear God's sayings from the Bible and that you do not let them depart from your eyes and that you keep them in the midst of your heart. May the Word of God that is alive and active be like a sword upon your lips that you will be driven to speak His Word continually. We say the angels of the Lord are activated to the sound of God's Word spoken from your mouth. May the living Word of God wash you, cleanse you, and fill you with faith. We prophesy that the Word of God shall permeate you with power, truth, and life in Jesus' Name!

SCRIPTURE

My son, attend to my words; incline thine ear unto my sayings. Let them not depart from thine eyes; keep them in the midst of thine heart. For they are life unto those that find them, and health to all their flesh. Keep thy heart with all diligence; for out of it are the issues of life (Proverbs 4:20-23).

JOURNAL

Write down a verse (or several verses) that bring you life today and fill you with faith.

The living Word
of God washes me,
cleanses me, and
fills me with faith.

ANTICIPATING HIS COMING

DECREE

We decree that you never lose sight of His glorious second coming! May you continue to anticipate the return of our Lord, for your redemption draws near. May those in this day who mock and ignore the day of the Lord's return have no ability to sway your focus and expectation to see Jesus. We break the power of all dimness of vision, distraction, and lethargy that would remove your eyes from your heavenly reward. May you be in line with the Scriptures that declare, "Come quickly, Lord Jesus!" We say you are found among the faithful saints who anticipate His appearing. We declare you are a vessel that is prepared with oil in your lamp awaiting the bridegroom. We decree you are one in whom the day of the Lord shall not overtake you as a thief, but that you will be ready and expectant at all times. May a renewed excitement for the Lord's soon return well up from within you and may the joy of His coming refresh you today!

SCRIPTURE

Nevertheless we, according to his promise, look for new heavens and a new earth, wherein dwelleth righteousness (2 Peter 3:13).

JOURNAL

Are you ready for Jesus to return? How can you live more prepared, whether He comes today or in 100 years from now?

I decree that I never lose sight of His glorious second coming!

ASSURED FAITH

DECREE

We decree you receive an assured faith that provides you the proof of the things you are hoping for and praying about. Through the eye of faith, we declare you are able to see the things that you cannot see with your natural eye. We break the power of all unbelief, doubt, fear, and faithlessness in the Name of Jesus. We speak to every opposing circumstance that would try to dissuade your confidence that what you are praying for shall manifest. We say your faith is unshakable and unmovable and becomes your proof of the facts. We prophesy that you know beyond any shadow of doubt that the Lord has heard your prayers, heaven is moving, and miracles are in motion. We say your faith shall be assured and you shall not be anxious for anything, but shall rest in the fact that your requests are being heard in the throne room of grace. We prophesy an assurance of faith to rest and remain upon you today!

SCRIPTURE

Now faith is the assurance (the confirmation, the title deed) *of the things [we] hope for, being the proof of things [we] do not see and the conviction of their reality [faith perceiving as real fact what is not revealed to the senses]* (Hebrews 11:1 AMPC).

JOURNAL

Have you ever struggled with doubt? Journal it and then write down some words of faith that counter it.

I know beyond any shadow of doubt that the Lord has heard my prayers. heaven is moving, and miracles are in motion.

A Sharp Memory

Decree

We decree you have a sharp and healthy memory. We declare your mind is able to recall and recount with accuracy and precision. We prophesy that your mind is blessed and that no condition or disorder affecting your memory shall ever affect you in Jesus' Name. We say all forms of dementia, Alzheimer's, amnesia, and memory loss are bound and any genetic disorders are halted. We speak that you are mindful, aware, and cognizant. May your memories begin to increase and expand in number. We say that all negative, haunting, and hurtful memories are replaced by positive memories that bring value to your future. We decree you are able to remember Scripture, truth, and the instructions of the Holy Spirit. We say you can remember all things you have learned through study and reading. We decree your mind and your memory are blessed and shall always function to their fullest capacity in the Name of Jesus!

Scripture

But the Comforter, which is the Holy Ghost, whom the Father will send in my name, he shall teach you all things, and bring all things to your remembrance, whatsoever I have said unto you (John 14:26).

Journal

What can you do today to exercise your memory?

My mind and my memory are blessed
and shall always function to their
fullest capacity in the *Name of Jesus!*

A COMPLETE WORK

DECREE

We decree that the work that Jesus has begun in your life shall be completed and not cut short. We say everything you are meant to become and all that you are called to do shall be finished. We declare that all intimidating spirits that would make you believe that you are not doing anything of significant value are bound in Jesus' Name. We say you carry upon you a finisher's anointing and that you have within you the ability to complete and finalize tasks. We declare you begin to see meaningful fruit for your labors. We say every effort to produce something profitable shall yield results. We prophesy your heavenly calling shall never be aborted and you shall finish all the work heaven has assigned you. We speak a new confidence to rest upon you regarding the good work of God being completed within you by Jesus Christ!

SCRIPTURE

Being confident of this very thing, that he which hath begun a good work in you will perform it until the day of Jesus Christ (Philippians 1:6).

JOURNAL

What work has Jesus begun in you? Journal the progress that you've made from the beginning until now, and thank Him for how much further He is going to take you.

FINISH

I carry a finisher's anointing and I have within me the ability to complete and finalize tasks.

Authority and Dominion

Decree

We decree that you rise up and take your rightful place of authority and dominion against the evils and darkness of this world. We say you shall not be intimidated by an antichrist spirit. We declare you tread boldly upon all the powers of the devil. We prophesy that you are well equipped to wage spiritual warfare and come out with a decisive win. We say that the prophetic words in your mouth are saturated with power. We say that you shall have the taste and grace upon your words to speak in places and regions that aren't receptive to the Word of God. We say you carry weightiness from the Spirit of God upon you. We say a new authority comes upon your prayer language and to your prayer life. May you walk in all the levels of dominion that Christ has established for you, and may you take your rightful place of divine rule in Jesus' Name!

Scripture

Behold, I give unto you power to tread on serpents and scorpions, and over all the power of the enemy: and nothing shall by any means hurt you (Luke 10:19).

Journal

Where has the Lord given you special authority? How are you claiming dominion for the Kingdom of God today?

I walk in all the levels of dominion that Christ has established for me. and I take my rightful place of divine rule in Jesus' Name!

THOUGHTS OF PURITY AND VIRTUE

DECREE

Today we speak a cleansing over your mind. We decree every thought is captive to the rule of Jesus Christ. We say all thoughts of impurity, godlessness, fear, and unbelief must dissipate. We say unhappy and undesirable imaginations must leave your mind and be replaced with that which is pure, lovely, life-giving, and filled with peace. We say that every attack of the enemy that would demonically come to bombard your thoughts with that which opposes truth and godliness are bound in the Name of Jesus. We command every evil thought to get out of your mind, be removed from your dreams, and go from your thinking. We call for a divine saturation of your mind and thoughts by the Spirit of the Lord. We decree you are able to think of a good outcome for every circumstance and that you have the capacity to imagine the light at the end of every tunnel. We prophesy that you can always picture a good report! We say your thoughts are pure, blessed, and filled with life in Jesus' Name!

SCRIPTURE

Finally, brethren, whatsoever things are true, whatsoever things are honest, whatsoever things are just, whatsoever things are pure, whatsoever things are lovely, whatsoever things are of good report; if there be any virtue, and if there be any praise, think on these things (Philippians 4:8).

JOURNAL

Today, choose a thought, idea, or subject that would pass the Philippians 4:8 criteria. Write it down and create a reminder for yourself to consider this topic throughout the day. (If you don't manage it today, keep trying until you succeed.) How do you feel at the end of a day of focusing on pure thoughts?

My thoughts are pure, blessed, and filled with life in Jesus' Name!

DECLARATION FOR FRIENDS AND FAMILY

DECREE

We decree today over all your friends and loved ones that they are overshadowed by the Spirit of the Lord. May the power of God rest tangibly upon them and they shall sense His presence. We declare they receive wisdom and revelation from the Lord. We say they hear God's voice. We prophesy they walk in divine health, live long lives, and receive God's protection. We say angels are released to encamp about them. We say your friends and loved ones shall serve the Lord and not fall away from Him. We prophesy that they walk in God's will and His divine plan for their lives. We speak that they shall find gainful employment and activity and shall enjoy life to the full. We take authority over every plot, plan, and scheme of the enemy that would try to come against your friends and loved ones. We say that devil cannot hold them in any form of bondage in Jesus' Name. We say they are well, and all is well concerning those you love!

SCRIPTURE

For God is my witness, whom I serve with my spirit in the gospel of his Son, that without ceasing I make mention of you always in my prayers (Romans 1:9).

JOURNAL

List several friends and loved ones, then write down how and where you envision the Lord working in their life.

My friends and loved ones are well,
and all is well concerning those I love!

IT WILL COME TO PASS!

DECREE

We decree that every prophetic word from God that has been spoken into your life shall come to pass without fail. We declare you have a steadfast confidence in the word of the Lord that has been given to you and that you are able to wage a good warfare with the prophecies that have gone before you. We say that you are able to stand firm in the prophetic word and are able to discern prophetic truth. We decree all words spoken that have not lined up biblically or been proven as legitimate will not carry any weight. We speak the words from God shall be pressed through to fruition and not stopped by the enemy. We say the word of the Lord over your life concerning your prophetic future shall come to pass and shall not be aborted in the Name of Jesus. We say, "It will come to pass!"

SCRIPTURE

This charge I commit unto thee, son Timothy, according to the prophecies which went before on thee, that thou by them mightest war a good warfare (1 Timothy 1:18).

JOURNAL

Journal the prophetic words that have been spoken over your life. Put a big check mark after *all* of them!

Every prophetic word from God that has been spoken into my life shall come to pass without fail.

A READY ANSWER

DECREE

We decree that within you lies the ability to give an answer to every person who would question you or ask a question of you. We say that you have the wisdom of the Lord upon your words to talk to any person who comes across your path or would ask you about things pertinent to the Kingdom of God. We prophesy that those who would come to you with hard questions will be able to receive answers from the wisdom of God that rests upon you. We speak that people shall seek you out to know the way of God and you will be able to help guide and lead them to the light. We say you have clear and decisive answers and that no spirit of confusion or perplexity shall be able to interfere with what you have to say. We say your tongue is as the pen of a ready writer able to give hope in due season and answers to a generation in need. We say the ready answers of God are in your mouth!

SCRIPTURE

But sanctify the Lord God in your hearts: and be ready always to give an answer to every man that asketh you a reason of the hope that is in you with meekness and fear (1 Peter 3:15).

JOURNAL

Write down a testimony from your own life of something Jesus has done. Remind yourself of this experience—your life is a witness! If someone asks you a question you don't know how to answer, share your experience!

I say the ready answers
of God are in my mouth!

Extraordinary and Unique Miracles

Decree

We decree that you receive and experience the unique miracles of God. Like the early church saw extraordinary miracles performed at the hands of Paul, may you encounter the miraculous works of God in your life. May you see unusual and uncommon miracles. May you be a witness of the signs and wonders that confirm God's Word in action. We say that every demonic power that would prevent you from seeing, operating in, or encountering the miraculous is bound in Jesus' Name. We speak that you interact with all the elements of His profound glory that are intended by the Holy Spirit. May unusual miracles affect your family, your personal life, occupation, finances, health, and home. We say that special miracles shall be regularly noted in your life and no man-made traditions shall keep them from manifesting. We prophesy that special and unique miracles shall be your experience and your portion in Jesus' Name!

Scripture

God did extraordinary miracles through Paul, so that even handkerchiefs and aprons that had touched him were taken to the sick, and their illnesses were cured and the evil spirits left them (Acts 19:11-12 NIV).

Journal

What is the most unusual miracle you have ever heard of? What is the most unique miracle that you have ever personally seen?

Special and unique miracles shall be my experience and my portion in Jesus' Name!

Soft and Gentle Words

Decree

We decree that you carry a gentle and soothing word within your speech. We say that you can speak decently and tastefully in all tense conversations. We break the power of the enemy that would pressure you to defend yourself excessively or react harshly. We speak that you have the ability to maintain a calm and collected demeanor with every person you speak to. We say that wrath, anger, violence, and antagonism shall never consume you as you interact with those who would oppose you. We say you are surrounded in a gentle, mannerly spirit. We speak that those around you will be softened by your considerate behavior. May the gentle and thoughtful words that come from your mouth change your hearers for the better and may your words turn away all wrath and fighting. We say a soft and gentle word is on your lips.

Scripture

A gentle answer turns away wrath, but a harsh word stirs up anger (Proverbs 15:1 NIV).

Journal

Draft out a gentle and loving answer that you can use in various situations. Memorize it—you might need it today!

I have the ability to maintain a calm and collected demeanor with every person I speak to.

NO MORE DISAPPOINTMENT

DECREE

We decree you shall not live in the realm of repeated or continual disappointment. We prophesy that you shall not look at your circumstances and brace for disappointment. We break the power of all repeat patterns of letdown, setback, and disillusion in Jesus' Name. We prophesy that you will not experience negative blow after blow regarding the things you are believing for. We declare thorns and thistles are replaced with fruitful blooms. We speak that you attain results and achievement that will bring delight to your soul. We declare you see a sudden shift for the better that will boost your morale and give a new sense of determination. We decree that "disappointment" will not need to have a place in your vocabulary regarding your current situation. Disappointment is turned into delight, and we speak that you will rejoice for your season of relief has come in the Name of Jesus!

SCRIPTURE

Instead of the thorn shall come up the fir tree, and instead of the brier shall come up the myrtle tree: and it shall be to the Lord for a name, for an everlasting sign that shall not be cut off (Isaiah 55:13).

JOURNAL

What has disappointed you recently (even the tiniest thing)? Bring it before Jesus and ask Him to turn this into a delight. Come back later and write down what He does!

Disappointment is turned into delight, and I will rejoice for my season of relief has come in the Name of Jesus!

AN ENDURING PATIENCE

DECREE

We decree that you possess the divine patience that heaven brings. We speak that you are steady and constant in doing the will of God. We prophesy that you are steadfast in awaiting your breakthroughs and answers to prayer. We say patience has its perfect work within you. We speak that you maintain the ability to exhibit self-control and fortitude. We break the power of that which would agitate you and frustrate you from reaching your goals. We bind the work of all demonic powers that would meddle with your steady endurance. We decree your faith shall not fail and you shall not resort to shortcuts and side roads that do not yield a bountiful harvest. We speak that you receive a divine patience from the Lord that enables you to stand strong in every promise without wavering. We say patience saturates your being and you will complete your objectives, receive answered prayer, and attain the prize of your high calling in Christ Jesus!

SCRIPTURE

For ye have need of patience, that, after ye have done the will of God, ye might receive the promise (Hebrews 10:36).

JOURNAL

Have you ever been tempted to take a shortcut or use your own methods to bring something about? Journal this and ask Jesus to forgive you. Return everything to His hands and His timing.

_____

_____

_____

_____

_____

_____

Patience saturates my being and I will complete my objectives, receive answered prayer, and attain the prize of my high calling in Christ Jesus!

THE ENEMY MUST FLEE!

DECREE

We decree all the plots, plans, and schemes of the enemy must leave your life and circumstances in the authority of Jesus' Name! We prophesy that no demonic entity is allowed to hang around your home, your property, or your family. We say every evil spirit must leave your mind and your body. We say that all demonic activity must be halted. Every witchcraft curse, spell, and hex is broken by the power of God in the Name of Jesus. We draw a bloodline of the blood of Jesus around you and all that concerns you, and we say the work of evil cannot cross that line. We prophesy that where the enemy has come through as a flood the Lord puts him to flight. We say that you rise up and resist all of the devil's activity, causing him to flee. We say to the powers of darkness, "Leave, in Jesus' Name, and never return!"

SCRIPTURE

Submit yourselves therefore to God. Resist the devil, and he will flee from you (James 4:7).

JOURNAL

Journal about something the enemy has tried to use to invade your home. No matter how big or small, write it down and then cross it out and place it under the Name of Jesus.

_____

_____

_____

_____

_____

_____

_____

_____

All the plots, plans, and schemes of the enemy must leave my life and circumstances in the authority of Jesus' Name!

HEAVENLY RAINS

DECREE

We decree that you begin to experience the heavenly rains of the Spirit. May you encounter the outpouring of the Spirit that causes you to be refreshed and transitioned into the next divine season for your life. We say another fruitful season comes upon you, enabling you to do things and go places that you have not before. We say your best season of growth begins to take place as a result of a spiritual rainy, well-watered season. We prophesy that the rain of God removes the impurities, leftovers, and debris from the former season. We call for the visitation of God to fall upon you as the rain, allowing you to see the intentions of God's heart, His mind, and His will. We speak against a spiritual drought and we break the work of the devouring locust and cankerworm in Jesus' Name. We decree you are transitioned out of the desert into an oasis. We declare you are able to see and hear God clearly just as you would distinctly hear the literal rain. We say God Himself comes and visits you as the rain!

SCRIPTURE

Then shall we know, if we follow on to know the Lord: his going forth is prepared as the morning; and he shall come unto us as the rain, as the latter and former rain unto the earth (Hosea 6:3).

JOURNAL

Is there any area of your life that feels dry, stagnant, or empty? Bring it before the Lord, asking for His rain to fall there.

_____

_____

_____

_____

_____

_____

I call for the visitation of God to fall upon me as the rain, allowing me to see the intentions of God's heart, His mind, and His will.

RIGHT ON TIME!

DECREE

We decree that you always operate and function in God's perfect timing. We say in every circumstance and season that you arrive and leave with punctuality. We declare you experience timeliness both in the spiritual and the natural realms. We break the powers of tardiness, lateness, and delinquency in Jesus' Name. We prophesy that you possess the proper time management skills in your daily activities and procrastination is broken from you. We also speak that you manage time correctly in spiritual things and we say that you will not hold on to a former season beyond it's time. We declare you transition into the next chapter of your life right on time. We declare that you hear the movement and inner workings of God's clock and are skilled to walk in step with Him. We prophesy that you are able to see time as God does. We also declare no more overdue blessings and breakthroughs and we break the spirit of delay! We say that nothing in your life is behind schedule and everything is on time!

SCRIPTURE

Look carefully then how you walk, not as unwise but as wise, making the best use of the time, because the days are evil (Ephesians 5:15-16 ESV).

JOURNAL

Write down the important times on your schedule today, and give each appointment to the Lord. Take Jesus with you to each one: "12:30 me and Jesus lunch with so-and-so."

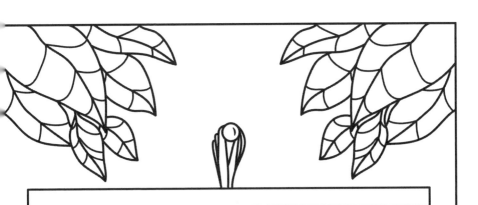

JANUARY

SUN	MON	TUE	WED	THU	FRI	SAT
1	2	3	4	5	6	7
8	9	10	11	12	13	14
15	16	17	18	19	20	21
22	23	24	25	26	27	28
29	30	31				

I say that nothing in my life is behind schedule and everything is on time!

PROMOTE HIS GOODNESS

DECREE

We decree you are able to see the good in all situations and circumstances. We speak that you will never be inclined to take the pessimistic approach. We say that you always look around you with an optimistic outlook. We speak that you don't emphasize the problem, but you are focused on the answer. We prophesy that you can look through every dark cloud and see the goodness of your God! We break any mental images of doom and gloom in Jesus' Name. We say that you look at this world through the eyes of God's redemptive plan and His mercy that triumphs over judgement. We say you see the good, promote the good, and show His goodness to the world. We declare that you are immersed in God's goodness to you and your family. We say that an anointing comes upon you to advocate everywhere you go that God is good and that His mercy endures forever!

SCRIPTURE

O give thanks unto the Lord; for he is good; for his mercy endureth for ever (1 Chronicles 16:34).

JOURNAL

Journal five ways you have seen God's goodness uniquely displayed in your life. Write down someone who might need to hear about this experience you have had.

I see the good, promote the good, and show His goodness to the world.

PEACE IN OUR HOME

DECREE

Today we decree that our home is filled with God's unsurpassable peace. The atmosphere is saturated with tranquility and serenity. We rely on the Lord's peace, which provides a sense of assurance in our minds and emotions. We declare that we are relaxed and calm. We break the powers of agitation, mayhem, chaos, and disarray in the Name of Jesus! We cast out any evil spirit that would bring disorder to the atmosphere. We declare that those who dwell in our home contribute to peace and do not give place to anything that would create turmoil. We speak that every person who enters our home is enveloped in heavenly peace. We say our home is a place where guests feel the Lord's supernatural rest upon them, and it opens the way for miracles in their lives. We speak great peace upon our home, in the mighty Name of Jesus!

SCRIPTURE

Now the Lord of peace himself give you peace always by all means. The Lord be with you all (2 Thessalonians 3:16).

JOURNAL

List the names of those who live in your home. After each person, give them a special title prophesying their destiny as part of a peaceful home (e.g., patient, studious, organized, settled, careful, gentle, forgiving).

_____

_____

_____

_____

_____

_____

_____

Today I decree that my home is filled with God's unsurpassable peace.

WE WILL SERVE THE LORD

DECREE

Today we declare that all who live in our home serve the Lord. We prophesy that each member of this household honors God in word, action, and deed. We are a family who gives the Lord the place of supreme rule, and we choose to uphold His Word and commandments. His Name shall always be reverenced under our roof. We speak words of praise and esteem about the Lord. We speak that in this home the Lord is high and lifted up, and His presence fills every room! We say that no antichrist spirit is able to operate in this house. We break the power of any opposing spirit or influence, and we close the door to all things that dishonor our God. We decree that the banner written upon the doorposts of this house is, "As for me and my house, we serve the Lord!"

SCRIPTURE

And if it seem evil unto you to serve the Lord, choose you this day whom ye will serve; whether the gods which your fathers served that were on the other side of the flood, or the gods of the Amorites, in whose land ye dwell: but as for me and my house, we will serve the Lord (Joshua 24:15).

JOURNAL

How do the members of your household serve Jesus in their own unique ways? If some don't right now, prophetically write down their destined role in His Kingdom. Pray over each one until God makes this clear to you.

TIME FOR TOGETHERNESS

DECREE

Today we declare that our home is filled with oneness, togetherness, unity, and fellowship. Our home is characterized by a closeness and affection between all who live and visit here. We love to be together, talk, interact, and communicate with one another. We are a family that enjoys fun activities without distraction or interruption. We say that nothing can disrupt our family time and the closeness we share in this home. We break the power of all evil spirits that would come to separate, divide, distract, or invade our togetherness, in Jesus' Name! We prophesy that we have our schedules, plans, and activities in order so that an atmosphere of unity thrives and we can spend time together without disruption or distraction. We say that we are a household of togetherness and we are a family of closeness!

SCRIPTURE

Behold, how good and how pleasant it is for brethren to dwell together in unity! (Psalm 133:1)

JOURNAL

What does your family most enjoy doing together? When will you make time to do this again?

My home is filled with oneness, togetherness, unity, and fellowship.

ABOUT BRENDA KUNNEMAN

Brenda Kunneman pastors Lord of Hosts Church in Omaha, Nebraska with her husband, Hank. She is a writer and teacher who ministers nationally and internationally, seeing lives change through the prophetic word and ministry in the Holy Spirit coupled with a balanced, relevant message. Together, she and her husband also host a weekly TV program, *New Level with Hank and Brenda*, on Daystar Television Network.